Illinois Law in the School Office:
The Essential Desk Reference

Brian D. Schwartz
Scott L. Day

Published by:

Illinois Principals Association
2940 Baker Drive
Springfield, Illinois 62703
www.ilprincipals.org
217-525-1383

First Printing,
May 2012

Cover Design by Maggie Day

ISBN 978-0-615-61032-0

Illinois Law in the School Office: The Essential Desk Reference. Copyright © 2012 by Brian D. Schwartz and Scott L. Day. All rights reserved. Printed in the United States of America. No part of this book may be used or reproduced in any manner whatsoever without written permission, except in the case of brief quotations embodied in critical articles and reviews. For information, contact the publisher, Illinois Principals Association, 2940 Baker Drive, Springfield, Illinois 62703 or 217-525-1383.

Legal Disclaimer

The ideas, suggestions and advice provided in this book are those of the authors. While every effort has been made to present sound and accurate legal and practical guidance, the information herein is not warranted and does not constitute legal advice. The reader should be aware that the field of education law is in a constant state of change. Additionally, the policies, practices and procedures of your school district may impact the information provided herein. Readers are strongly encouraged to check with legal counsel before undertaking any decision that may require legal guidance or implementing or adopting any policy, procedure or practice.

About the Authors

Brian D. Schwartz has practiced school law for fifteen years. Brian strives to provide his clients with sound, practical legal advice that is geared toward solving problems, not creating them.

In addition to maintaining an active private practice, Brian serves as the associate director and general counsel to the Illinois Principals Association. He is also an adjunct professor at the University of Illinois at Springfield, where he teaches several graduate courses on school and employment law.

Brian is the author of two books: The Law of Homeschooling (2008) and Finding Middle Ground in K-12 Education (2009). He has also written numerous book chapters, law review articles and scholarly publications.

Brian previously served on the national board of directors of the Education Law Association and is the past chair of the Illinois State Bar Association's Education Law Section Council. He is a member of the Illinois and National Council of School Attorneys.

Brian is a popular speaker and presenter and has spoken nationally and internationally on issues pertaining to school law. For more information, visit his website at www.edlawyer.org.

Scott L. Day is Associate Professor and Chair of the Department of Educational Leadership at the University of Illinois at Springfield. He earned his Ed. D. in Educational Organization and Leadership from the University of Illinois at Urbana-Champaign in 2000. Dr. Day was awarded the Outstanding Dissertation Award from the University of Illinois' chapter of Phi Delta Kappa in 2000.

Before coming to UIS in 1997, Dr. Day spent thirteen years as Middle School Assistant Principal in Pennsylvania and Junior High School Principal in St. Joseph, Illinois. In 2010, Professor Day was awarded the Pearson Faculty Award for Outstanding Teaching at the University of Illinois at Springfield. Dr. Day currently teaches courses in the areas of school improvement and instructional leadership. Dr. Day has developed and taught an instructional design course online in the Master Teacher Leadership program for the last ten years. His previous research publications includes work on blended learning, using design-based research to improve online courses and programmatic change, technology uses of at-risk students and school district reorganization issues.

Dedications & Acknowledgements

There are a number of people who have supported me in the writing of this book. I am especially grateful to my parents, Annette and Jerry Schwartz, IPA Executive Director Jason Leahy, Marcy Dutton, Wally Mechtoldt and Dana Kinley.

To Professor Steven D. Rittenmeyer, my favorite college professor,
who always made the law fun and exciting.
— *Brian D. Schwartz*

To my family, for their continued love and support.
To Professor Thomas L. Mc Greal, a great professor and mentor.
— *Scott L. Day*

Additional thanks to Meagan Anderson and Dana Kinley for their proofreading skills.

Table of Contents

Chapter 1   Understanding the Law
    1.1   Introduction 1
    1.2   The Basics of a Lawsuit 1
    1.3   Acting as the Reasonable Employee 2
    1.4   Staying within the Course and Scope of Your Duties 3
    1.5   Immunity from Liability 4
    1.6   Mandated Reporter Status 4

    FAQs 6
    References 8

Chapter 2   The School Office: First Line of Contact
    2.1   Introduction 9
    2.2   Phone Calls and Phone Etiquette 9
    2.3   Visitors to the School: Assuring Order and Student Safety 10
    2.4   Effectively Dealing with Members of the Public 11
    2.5   Working with the Certified Teaching Staff 11
    2.6   Establishing Open Communication with the Principal and Supervisors ... 12
    2.7   Compliance with Copyright Laws When Reproducing Documents 12
    2.8   The Freedom of Information Act 12
    2.9   Fire and Safety Drill Requirements 13
    2.10   Sex Offenders at School 14
    2.11   Animals on School Property 15

    FAQs 16
    Checklists and Sample Forms 19
    References 22

Chapter 3   Residency, Enrollment and Withdrawal
    3.1   Introduction 25
    3.2   Proof of Residency 26
    3.3   Other Enrollment Factors and Criteria 26
    3.4   Students Who Move During the School Year 27
    3.5   Homeless Students 27
    3.6   Foster Children 28
    3.7   Military Families 28
    3.8   Illegal Aliens 28
    3.9   Students Receiving Special Education Services 28
    3.10   Students Who Are Not Residents of the District 29
    3.11   The Tuition Option 29
    3.12   Truancy 30
    3.13   Withdrawal from School 30
    3.14   Special Circumstances Impacting Enrollment 30

FAQs 31
Checklists and Sample Forms 33
References 40

Chapter 4   Safeguarding and Maintaining Student Records
    4.1   Introduction 47
    4.2   A Parent's Right to Access and Control the Student Record 48
    4.3   The School's Obligation to Safeguard and Secure Student Records 49
    4.4   The Records Custodian 50
    4.5   Fees to Copy Records 50
    4.6   Transfer of Student Records to Another School District 50
    4.7   Transfer Student Records to Third Parties 51
    4.8   Students Who Are 18 51
    4.9   Dealing with Divorced Parents 51
    4.10   Former Students 52
    4.11   Electronic Grade Books 52
    4.12   Student Biometric Information 52
    4.13   Requests from the Military and Institutions of Higher Learning 52
    4.14   Permanent and Temporary Records 52
    4.15   Destruction of Records 53

FAQs 54
Sample Forms 57
References 61

Chapter 5   Managing Student Medical Needs and Medications
    5.1   Student Medication in General 71
    5.2   The Role of Support Staff in Handing Student Medical Needs 71
    5.3   Administration of Medication at School 72
    5.4   Prescription v. Non-Prescription Medication 72
    5.5   Self-Administration of Medication by Students 73
    5.6   Diabetic Students 73
    5.7   Emergency Medical Aid to Students 73
    5.8   Storage and Maintenance of Medication 73
    5.9   Notification to Parents and Students 73
    5.10   Student Record Entries 73

FAQs 75
Checklists and Sample Forms 77
References 84

Chapter 6   Immunizations, Health, Dental and Vision Requirements
    6.1   Introduction 91
    6.2   Health Examination Requirements 91
    6.3   Required Immunizations 92

6.4	Dental Examinations	92
6.5	Eye Examinations	92
6.6	Exemptions and Waivers	93
6.7	Homeless Students	93

FAQs 94
Checklists and Sample Forms 96
References 104

Chapter 7 Special Student Populations

7.1	Introduction	111
7.2	Special Education	111
7.3	Section 504 of the Rehabilitation Act of 1973	112
7.4	Response to Intervention	113
7.5	Low Income Students and Families	114
7.6	Homeless Students	115
7.7	Foster Children	115
7.8	Undocumented Students	115
7.9	Homeschool Students	116
7.10	Students with Special Religious Needs	117

FAQs 118
Checklists and Sample Forms 121
References 124

Chapter 8 Handling Money and School Account Management

8.1	Introduction	127
8.2	Basic Money Management	127
8.3	Handling Cash from Events and Fundraisers	128
8.4	Student Activity Accounts	128
8.5	Petty Cash Accounts	129
8.6	Revolving Fund Accounts	129
8.7	Credit Cards and Procurement Cards	130

FAQs 131
Checklists 132
References 133

Chapter 9 Transportation and Related Issues

9.1	Introduction	137
9.2	Types of Allowable Transportation	137
9.3	Pupil Transportation Reimbursement	138
9.4	Transportation of Homeless Students	138
9.5	Transportation of Students with Disabilities.	139
9.6	School Bus Communication Devices	139

9.7	Bus Pre-Trip and Post-Trip Inspection	139
9.8	Post Bus Accident Procedures	140

FAQs 141
Checklists and Sample Forms 143
References 150

Chapter 10   Employment Issues and Rights of Non-Certified Staff

10.1	Introduction	155
10.2	Personnel Records	156
10.3	Evaluation	156
10.4	Discipline and Dismissal	157
10.5	Overtime Compensation	157
10.6	Religious Holidays	157
10.7	Freedom from Workplace Harassment	157
10.8	Nursing Mothers in the Workplace	157
10.9	Americans with Disabilities Act	157
10.10	Family and Medical Leave Act	158
10.11	Whistleblower Protection	158
10.12	Employee Credit Privacy Act	158
10.13	Equal Pay Act	159
10.14	School Visitation Act	159
10.15	Prohibited Political Activities	159
10.16	Gift Ban Act	159
10.17	Conflicts of Interest	160
10.18	Use of School District Email Accounts	160
10.19	Outside Employment	160

FAQs 161
References 164

Index 171

Introduction

Working in a school is both rewarding and tough. School secretaries, nurses, aides, receptionists, custodians, bus drivers and a host of others assure that our schools are run efficiently and that children are the top priority. These talented individuals answer questions from parents, manage student medication, fix whatever needs to be fixed, assure that student records are accurately maintained, assist teachers with a variety of needs, coordinate school safety drills, enroll and withdraw students, assist with special education issues, handle school finances, transport students to and from school and school activities and do whatever else is needed.

This book is our effort to make the life of these busy individuals a little more manageable. In doing so, we have consulted with a number of school support professionals about the areas of law and policy that they deal with on a routine basis. From there, we organized this book into ten chapters. Each chapter contains detailed narratives on relevant issues, frequently asked questions and commonly used forms and resources.

As such, Illinois Law in the School Office is a one stop, essential desk reference for busy school support professionals.

If you are a school support professional, we thank you for the work that you do and we hope that you find this book a worthwhile resource. If you are a principal or superintendent, we encourage you to make sure that a copy of this book is in each school office, as it will prove to be an invaluable resource for everyone (including you) who deals with parents, students and the public on a daily basis.

– Brian D. Schwartz & Scott L. Day

Chapter 1

Understanding the Law

"If you laid all of our laws end to end, there would be no end."
– Mark Twain

In This Chapter:

1.1   Introduction
1.2   The Basics of a Lawsuit
1.3   Acting as the Reasonable Employee
1.4   Staying Within the Course and Scope of Your Duties
1.5   Immunity from Liability
1.6   Mandated Reporter Status

FAQs
References

1.1 Introduction

In today's litigious society, it is more important than ever to understand the law. This is true because:

1. Anyone can easily and inexpensively file a lawsuit.
2. Failure to know and understand the law is not a defense.

Based on the above statements, the purpose of this chapter is not to scare you. It is to make you aware of the basic laws and procedures that fall within the responsibilities of school support professionals. As you will read later in this chapter, school employees who stay within the course and scope of their duties and act in a reasonable manner MUST be defended by the school district in the event of a lawsuit against the employee. The school district is required to pay all attorney fees, costs of the lawsuit and damages.

However, if a school employee fails to act reasonably or fails to stay within the course and scope of his or her duties, the employee may have to pay for all costs of the lawsuit out of his or her own pocket.

To fully appreciate the scope of this problem – and how to avoid it – it is helpful to understand the basic anatomy of a lawsuit.

1.2 The Basics of a Lawsuit

When a student is injured (emotionally or physically) parents sometimes file a lawsuit in the name of their child. (A parent or guardian must actually file the lawsuit because the child is a minor and cannot initiate the lawsuit in his or her own name.) When the lawsuit is filed, it is a standard legal practice to sue all parties who may have had an involvement in the situation, including school support staff.

For example, suppose that a student becomes ill after being given the wrong medication by the school secretary. The ensuing lawsuit may include as defendants the school secretary (who gave the student the wrong medication), the school nurse (who is in charge of student medical needs), the principal (who is responsible for supervising the secretary and nurse), the superintendent (who is the chief executive officer of the district) and members of the school board (who are ultimately responsible for things that happen in the school district).

When a lawsuit is filed, the attorneys for both sides will attempt to determine if the school employees acted reasonably and stayed within the course and scope of their duties. If it is determined that the employees acted reasonably and were performing the duties they were hired to perform, then the school district must pay for the entire cost of the lawsuit, including damages. However, if it is determined that any employee failed to act reasonably or stepped outside his or her duties, that employee must defend himself or herself and pay all damages!

Again, in terms of an example, let us envision that a group of students are playing a game of "dodgeball" before the start of school. Let's further assume that the school's playground supervisor decides to participate in the game, hits a child with a ball and the child is injured. If the parents file a lawsuit against the playground supervisor, attorneys will attempt to determine if the employee was acting reasonably and in the course and scope of her duties. This can be a difficult task, as it could be argued that the employee was supervising the students while interacting with them. However, on the other side of the coin, it could be argued that the employee crossed a line and went from supervising the students to playing with them, which is not a part of her job and is not reasonable.

It is important to determine if an employee is acting reasonably and within the course and scope of his or her job guidelines, as the answer to this question frequently determines who pays the costs of the lawsuit and any resulting damages. If it is determined that the employee was performing his or her job in a reasonable fashion, the school district is obligated to provide representation to the employee and pay any and all damages that may result. If the interests of the employee are not the same as the interests of the school district, the employee can usually request that the district pay for separate counsel for the employee, instead of having the school district's attorney represent both parties.

If, however, it is determined that the employee stepped outside his or her job duties or failed to act in a reasonable fashion, the employee is generally responsible for obtaining his or her own attorney and paying for all costs of the lawsuit – including damages – out of his or her own pocket!

1.3 Acting as the Reasonable Employee

Again, under the theory that anyone can file a lawsuit, the aim of this chapter is to help school employees protect themselves, so that any lawsuit is handled at the school district's expense and not at the individual's expense. It is therefore important to explore in greater depth what it means for school employees to: (1) stay within the course and scope of their duties; and (2) perform these functions in a reasonable manner.

We will start with what it means to act as the reasonable employee. This obligation requires school employees to act as the "reasonable person" would act in his or her position and under the particular circumstances. For example, a teacher is held to the standard of a reasonable teacher, a nurse to the standard of a reasonable nurse and a playground supervisor to the standard of a reasonable playground supervisor, and so forth.

What we have found is that most school employees are reasonable people and hold themselves out accordingly. Perhaps the one area where reasonableness goes out the window is when dealing with students who are not behaving properly. Take for example two students who get into a fight on school property. What it means to act reasonably depends on whether the school employee attempts to break up the fight or prefers to handle the situation through different means.

If an employee does attempt to physically break up a student fight, the employee should use no more force than is necessary to address the situation. Once the students are separated and the situation is abated from a safety standpoint, the employee should refrain from making further physical contact with the students. In cases where a school employee fears for his or her own safety and does not want to get between the students, the reasonable thing to do is direct the students to stop fighting, call for assistance and keep other students out of the conflict.

Likewise, if a student begins arguing or yelling at a school employee, the reasonable thing to do in these circumstances is to deescalate the situation or walk away. It is inherently unreasonable for a school employee (who is an adult) to get into a verbal or physical altercation with a student.

1.4 Staying Within the Course and Scope of Your Duties

It is extremely important for a school employee to know the exact requirements of his or her job, as stepping outside the employee's specific job function could lead to personal liability! Job duties are found in places such as school and district policy manuals, collective bargaining agreements and individual contracts. Every employee should have a job description.

If a school employee ever has a question as to whether or not a certain function falls within his or her job duties, it is important to seek guidance from a supervisor. For example, let's assume that the school secretary is driving to school one cold and snowy day and sees a young student who has missed her bus. The student is attempting to walk to school but the snow and wind are quickly turning her into a snowperson. Most of us (we hope) would not simply wave as we drive by, but would want to help the student get to school. However, after reading the above paragraphs, you should be asking yourself if transporting the student to school falls within your job duties. Since most secretaries are not bus drivers, this question deserves serious consideration.

With these cold, hard facts (no pun intended), the secretary has a choice to make. Leave the student to her own means, hoping that she does not freeze to death, or pick up the student and risk being held personally liable if the student is somehow injured in the course of the secretary transporting her to school. In looking at this situation, there is middle ground. Since most of us have cell phones (if you don't you can generally borrow one from the student), the secretary could place a call to the school and seek permission from the principal or superintendent to bring the student to school. If permission is granted, then transporting the student becomes a de facto job duty of the secretary, and she is covered legally if the student is injured on the way to school.

The bottom line is therefore: If you don't know if you should be doing something, ASK! If you are granted permission, you are protected if a student is subsequently injured.

1.5 Immunity from Liability

At this point, you may be wondering how a school district defends itself and its employees in the case where a lawsuit is filed. However, it might be more important to ask how a school district is able to stay in business with so many opportunities for the school district and school employees to be sued. After all, it seems like everyone has an attorney today and defending against a lawsuit – even a frivolous one – is an expensive and time-consuming proposition.

Because school districts are deemed to have "deep pockets" (and are therefore a frequent target of lawsuits) and because schools are funded with taxpayer money, the State Legislature has enacted safeguards to help prevent school districts and school employees from being successfully sued every time a student is injured. One of these "immunity" protection laws provides that school employees stand *"in loco parentis"* or in place of the student's parents. Here, school employees "may use reasonable force as needed to maintain safety for the other students, school personnel or persons or for the purpose of self defense or the defense of property." If a student is injured, the *in loco parentis* protection protects the school and employees from successfully being sued. However, it should be remembered that the *in loco parentis* immunity has limitations, mainly that school employees cannot use corporal punishment as a method of student discipline.

Another important immunity protects decision-makers from liability for judgments that they must make as part of their day-to-day duties. Take for example a relatively recent case in Illinois where a student was injured in a car crash. The student was a new driver and asked the principal if he could leave school early due to deteriorating winter weather conditions. The principal refused the student's request and sent him back to class. When school was eventually dismissed at its regular time, the weather had made the roads even more hazardous and the student was involved in a personal injury crash on the way home from school. The student's parents instituted a lawsuit (remember anyone can sue you), but the Illinois Supreme Court eventually dismissed the suit based on a provision in the State's Tort Immunity Act, which protects employees for discretionary decisions in the scope of their employment. The Court reasoned that the principal had made a discretionary decision not to let the student leave early and was therefore protected.

The above case again demonstrates the aforementioned important point: If you are not sure whether you should be doing something as part of your duties, ask your supervisor. If your supervisor approves you performing the duty, you are protected. Likewise, your supervisor is protected because he or she made a discretionary decision as part of his or her supervisory duties.

1.6 Mandated Reporter Status

In Illinois, mandated reporters are obligated to contact the Department of Children and Family Services or DCFS whenever there is reasonable cause to believe that a child has been abused or neglected by a parent or caregiver. Mandated reporters include teachers, school personnel, educational advocates assigned to a child pursuant to the School Code, truant officers, directors and staff assistants of day care centers and nursery schools and child care workers. School support staff members are included in the above definition and are required to report suspected cases of child abuse and neglect.

Reports are made through a special hotline, which can be reached at 800-25-ABUSE (800-252-2873).

Note, all reports must be made immediately upon becoming aware of suspected abuse or neglect by a parent or caregiver. Furthermore, all school personnel who have first hand information of the suspected abuse or neglect must either make the report to DCFS themselves or must have their names included in the DCFS report.

Failure to report suspected child abuse or neglect is punishable by law. Therefore, if you have any indication that abuse or neglect may have occurred, you should contact DCFS. DCFS will then make a decision as to whether or not to pursue the situation.

FAQs

Can I be sued?
Anyone can be sued; however, if you were performing your job duties in a reasonable manner, the school district is obligated to defend you, including paying for your attorney and all costs of the lawsuit.

How will I know if I am part of a lawsuit against the school district?
If you are a party to a lawsuit, you will be personally served with a copy of the lawsuit either by the local sheriff's office or a process server. In certain circumstances, the school district's attorney may accept service of the lawsuit on your behalf, but the attorney will immediately notify you of this fact.

Will the school district defend me if I am sued for something that happened at work?
If you stay within the course and scope of your duties and act in a reasonable manner, the school district must defend you and must pay all attorney fees, costs of the lawsuit and damages.

What does it mean to act as a reasonable school employee?
This obligation requires school employees to act as the 'reasonable person" would act in his or her position and under the particular circumstances. For example, a teacher is held to the standard of a reasonable teacher, a nurse to the standard of a reasonable nurse and a playground supervisor to the standard of a reasonable playground supervisor, and so forth. For more information, see Section 1.3.

Should I have a job description?
It is recommended that every employee have a job description that specifically outlines and explains all job duties and expectations.

What should I do if I am not sure whether or not something is part of my job?
If you are ever unsure whether a task falls within your job duties, make sure to ask your supervisor. If your supervisor approves you completing the task it becomes a de facto job duty and you are protected if there is ever a lawsuit.

What should I do if I am named as a defendant in the lawsuit?
You should immediately contact the school district's attorney. This individual will advise you of the next steps in the process. Note that if you ever feel that the school district's attorney is not properly representing your interests you should ask for a separate attorney to be appointed to represent your needs. If you are a member of a union, you should also notify your union, as the union will be extremely helpful in walking you though this process.

Should I contact DCFS if I think child abuse or neglect might have taken place, but I'm not sure?

Yes. Whenever you have reasonable cause to believe that abuse or neglect has occurred you should contact the DCFS hotline. A hotline operator will take down the information and DCFS will then make a determination as to whether or not to pursue the matter.

Where should I report suspected child abuse or neglect?

Reports are made through a special hotline, which can be reached at 800-25-ABUSE (800-252-2873).

Can I share with the building principal the specifics of the DCFS call?

Yes, as long as the principal is not the one suspected of abusing or neglecting the child. However, telling the school principal about the suspected abuse or neglect does not relieve you of your responsibility to personally call the DCFS hotline.

References

105 ILCS 5/24/24. Maintenance of discipline.

Subject to the limitations of all policies established or adopted under Section 14-8.05, teachers, other certificated educational employees, and any other person, whether or not a certificated employee, providing a related service for or with respect to a student shall maintain discipline in the schools, including school grounds which are owned or leased by the board and used for school purposes and activities. In all matters relating to the discipline in and conduct of the schools and the school children, they stand in the relation of parents and guardians to the pupils. This relationship shall extend to all activities connected with the school program, including all athletic and extracurricular programs, and may be exercised at any time for the safety and supervision of the pupils in the absence of their parents or guardians.

Nothing in this Section affects the power of the board to establish rules with respect to discipline; except that each board shall establish a policy on discipline, and the policy so established shall provide, subject to the limitations of all policies established or adopted under Section 14-8.05, that a teacher, other certificated employee, and any other person, whether or not a certificated employee, providing a related service for or with respect to a student may use reasonable force as needed to maintain safety for the other students, school personnel or persons or for the purpose of self defense or the defense of property, shall provide that a teacher may remove a student from the classroom for disruptive behavior, and shall include provisions which provide due process to students. The policy shall not include slapping, paddling or prolonged maintenance of students in physically painful positions nor shall it include the intentional infliction of bodily harm.

The board may make and enforce reasonable rules of conduct and sportsmanship for athletic and extracurricular school events. Any person who violates such rules may be denied admission to school events for not more than one year, provided that written 10 days notice of the violation is given such person and a hearing had thereon by the board pursuant to its rules and regulations. The administration of any school may sign complaints as agents of the school against persons committing any offense at school events.

Chapter 2

The School Office: First Line of Contact

"Extraordinary events call for extraordinary actions."
– Dwight Schrute

In This Chapter:

2.1 Introduction
2.2 Phone Calls and Phone Etiquette
2.3 Visitors to the School: Assuring Order and Student Safety
2.4 Effectively Dealing with Members of the Public
2.5 Working with the Certified Teaching Staff
2.6 Establishing Open Communication with the Principal and Supervisors
2.7 Complying with Copyright Laws When Reproducing Documents
2.8 The Freedom of Information Act
2.9 Fire and Safety Drill Requirements
2.10 Sex Offenders at School
2.11 Animals on School Property

FAQs
Checklists and Sample Forms
References

2.1 Introduction

In order to present your school in a positive and professional light with the community, parents and anyone else who may come through the door, it is critical to develop a protocol (a script of sorts) for how to deal with everyday situations and, at the same time, maintain consistency in your responses to similar issues. Whether by phone, email or in person, how you handle visitors is an important part of your job. Next to the building administrator, office support staff works with the widest variety of people. With a multitude of personalities and needs, it is important to have a plan and follow it carefully. Moving away from the established plan may make a bad situation worse and may cause someone to look negatively on your school and staff.

2.2 Phone Calls and Phone Etiquette

One of the best secretaries we know is a former executive secretary for a large corporation. Why is she successful? You could say it has something to do with her previous work at a large corporation, or you could say it has everything to do with her workplace demeanor and training. She is professional in her attire and in the manner she speaks to everyone (parents, students, teachers and administrators alike) and she is extremely calm and well-organized. When observing her phone etiquette, she always sounds engaged and sympathetic to parents, while carefully listening to make sure that she understands the issue or circumstance. She often sounds like a caring parent when students share their problems, and she never uses sarcasm and never makes anyone feel as if they are wasting her time. If she does not know the answer, she promises to get back with the caller or visitor.

With the addition of voice mail and answering systems in schools today, we have experienced some very impersonal service when calling a school. When a person calls your office and asks for the principal, do not automatically send the caller to voice mail without indicating that the principal is not available at the time. Also, a secretary who listens intently will have the capacity to help diffuse a situation before it gets to a teacher or administrator. If you practice the techniques discussed above, you will soon build a positive rapport with parents, teachers, administrators and the public. Indeed, a good listener is someone the public can trust. Your performance is critical in helping the school maintain a positive relationship with the community.

2.3 Visitors to the School: Assuring Order and Student Safety

Many new school facilities are now designed to lock down the doors and only allow entrance through the main office. This design has enabled schools to monitor all traffic in and out of the building. A higher level of school safety was prompted by an increase in school intrusions by outsiders, child abduction cases and an increase of illegal activity around schools. In many cases, schools have become "safe havens" for students with less than desirable home situations. Without assuring proper order and safety plans, students and teachers find it most difficult to focus on teaching and learning activities.

In the case of older school buildings, a plan to re-route traffic in and out of a building is critical to ensure the safety of everyone. Due to fire safety exit requirements, schools are notorious for having doors that are hard to monitor. It is particularly difficult to keep doors locked and monitored when the weather is warm and the school is without air conditioning.

Here are a few suggestions to consider in developing a safety procedure for school visitors:

1. Develop a plan to establish one main entrance for everyone. A "sign-in" table may be needed to funnel people through the main office door.
2. Develop stringent "sign-in" and "sign-out" systems, which include name tag identification for all visitors. The tag should be brightly colored and easy to identify a visitor from a distance.
3. Set up a monitoring system utilizing custodial staff, teachers on hall duty, police liaison officers and security personnel to constantly monitor outside doors left ajar.
4. Develop lockdown procedures when alerted by the office.
5. Make sure classroom doors can be locked in a quick fashion in the case of an emergency.
6. Train students (practice drills) so they know why a lockdown may be necessary. Help students to remain calm in the event of an emergency.

7. Collect data on the problems that arise and conduct periodic evaluations so issues can be remedied to avoid a serious issue down the road.
8. Invite law enforcement agencies into your school to evaluate your plan. Solicit their feedback on issues as they arise.

For more information on school safety drill requirements, see Section 2.9, below.

2.4 Effectively Dealing with Members of the Public

The most important job of school office personnel is working on the day-to-day issues that may arise with parents, students and community members. Greeting people in a friendly way as they enter the office is the first sign of the type of service you provide. If you have a counter to block access to other parts of the office, be sure to stand and move to the counter. If you remain seated and talk from across the room, the body language you project may send the message that you are not interested in providing assistance. Your demeanor is the key to your success in any school setting.

When the community is present, be aware of the type of information you give out to others in their presence. In our experiences in visiting schools, we have heard too much confidential information about students and teachers being discussed in the main office area. Any information regarding a student or a teacher should be considered confidential and should not be discussed in earshot of the public. In small office settings, it may be necessary to have a phone in a more private area away from the public when phone calls of a confidential nature are made.

2.5 Working with the Certified Teaching Staff

Teachers in your building need the support of the office staff in many ways. Your role is very important in providing assistance to all personnel in the building. The school administration should assist you in developing procedures that the staff will follow to foster good communication, which in turn will help develop a good working relationship. Below you will find discussion questions that will help foster good communication and a positive working relationship.

1. What procedures will we use in completing attendance for the day?
2. Will the intercom be used during instruction time when a student needs to be sent to the office?
3. When will teachers receive phone calls that come in during the school day? Lunch time or after school?
4. What is the procedure for getting assistance to a classroom?
5. How will teachers be contacted in the event of an emergency?

Another consideration in working with certified staff is providing proper support for substitute teachers. One method that has been successful is greeting all substitutes with a folder outlining the school's bell schedule, basic procedures and a contact person near their room assignment to assist as questions arise. This folder of information is a good supplement to the teacher's specific lesson plans, daily schedule and activities. It is also a nice gesture if you or the building principal can escort the teacher to his or her room to help get the day off to a good start.

2.6 Establishing Open Communication with the Principal and Supervisors

Establishing open communication with your direct supervisor and other building administrators is imperative to your success and happiness on the job. Hopefully, your building administrator will initiate and schedule regular, short meetings with the office staff to communicate issues at the office and school level. It is also important that you have a voice in providing suggestions for improving the day-to-day workings of the office. If you are not getting the communication you need, the best practice is to ask your boss how he or she prefers to receive communications from you. It could be a simple drop in each morning, an email outlining areas that need attention, a note on his or her desk, a phone call or a voice mail.

2.7 Complying with Copyright Laws When Reproducing Documents

Copyright law extends to all original works of authorship, including software programs, CD-ROM and web pages. Additionally, it is no longer required that an author place notice on the document or register it in order to receive all of the rights enumerated by the Federal Copyright Act.

There are two important exceptions to the Copyright Act as it applies to the educational setting. The fair use doctrine provides that the fair use of a copyrighted work, including making copies (paper or digital) for purposes such as criticism, comment, news reporting, teaching (including multiple copies for classroom use), scholarship or research is not an infringement of copyright. There are four specific factors to be applied in determining whether or not a particular use violates copyright law: (1) the purpose and character of the use, including whether such use is of a commercial nature or is for nonprofit educational purposes; (2) the nature of the copyrighted work; (3) the amount and substantiality of the portion used in relation to the copyrighted work as a whole; and (4) the effect of the use upon the potential market for or value of the copyrighted work.

Public schools also benefit from three exemptions under the copyright law: face-to-face teaching at nonprofit educational institutions, educational broadcasting and not-for-profit performances. In the first exception, instructors may generally read, perform or display copyrighted material in a face-to-face address. Instructional broadcasting allows the performance of a non-dramatic literary or musical work for instructional purposes. Not-for-profit performances allow for the non-public performance of non-dramatic literary or musical works that are not for monetary gain.

The Copyright Act is very confusing and somewhat subjective. Therefore, it is suggested that you consult with your principal prior to making copies: (1) that comprise more than 10 percent of a book, article or work; (2) that comprise more than one chapter of a book, article or work; (3) that will be sold to students; (4) of movies or videos that will be shown to students for entertainment (as opposed to educational) purposes; or (5) that will be used outside a teacher's regular classes or class activities.

2.8 The Freedom of Information Act

The Freedom of Information Act, commonly referred to as FOIA, is a State law that is aimed at giving the public access to government (including school and school district) records. It is a means of providing oversight and assuring voters that governmental entities are complying with laws as well as internal policies and procedures.

In general, FOIA provides that if a member of the public makes a "FOIA request" for public records, a school district has five business days to respond, unless the documents are exempt from disclosure. For a partial list of valid disclosure exemptions, see Checklist 2-1. Notice of denial of a FOIA request must be provided in writing to the party requesting the information.

In certain hardship cases, a school district may obtain an additional five days to respond to a FOIA request. For a list of valid hardship reasons to extend the FOIA request deadline, see Checklist 2-2.

A school or district can charge fifteen cents per page to reproduce requested documents; however, the first 50 pages (black and white only) must be provided free of charge. If documents are requested in an electronic format, the school must attempt to comply with this request, and may charge the actual cost of reproducing the documents in the electronic format. Documents must be provided free of charge or at a reduced price if the requesting party states, and the school district confirms, that disclosure is "in the public interest."

Willful failure to comply with FOIA can lead to a civil penalty of up to $5,000. For additional information, contact your school district's freedom of information officer.

2.9 Fire and Safety Drill Requirements

The School Safety Drill Act was signed into law, effective August 1, 2005. Its purpose is to have public and private schools review their safety plans with first responders and to conduct safety drills. First responders include law enforcement, fire departments and fire districts. Listed below are the minimum State safety drill requirements for Illinois.

Fire Evacuation Drills:

The School Code requires school districts to conduct a minimum of three school evacuation drills each academic year to prepare students and school personnel for fire incidents.

Fire department participation is required for one of the three school evacuation drills each school year. The following dates are provided in order to arrange the participation of your local fire department or fire protection district:

September 1: Each fire department or fire district must contact the appropriate school administrator or his or her designee no later than September 1 of each year to arrange a date for the school evacuation fire drill.

September 15: Each school administrator or his or her designee must contact the responding local fire official no later than September 15 of each year and propose four dates within the month of October, during at least two different weeks of October, on which the drill shall occur. The fire official may choose any of the four dates, and if he or she does so, the drill shall occur on that date.

Upon participation of the local fire service, the appropriate local fire official shall certify the school evacuation drill was conducted.

When scheduling the evacuation drill, the school administrator or his or her designee and the local fire official may, by mutual agreement prior to September 14, choose to waive certain requirements.

Bus Evacuation Drill:
Schools must conduct a minimum of one bus evacuation drill each year. This drill must be incorporated into the curriculum in all public schools and in all other educational institution in this State that are supported or maintained, in whole or in part, by public funds and that provide instruction in any of the grades K-12. This curriculum must include instruction in safe bus riding practices for all students.

Law Enforcement Drill:
Schools must conduct a law enforcement drill each year to address certain incidents, including reverse evacuation, lock-downs, shootings, bomb threats and hazardous materials. Such drills must be conducted according to the school district's emergency or crisis response plans, protocols and procedures, with the participation of the appropriate law enforcement agency. Law enforcement drills may be conducted on days when students are not present in the school building.

Law enforcement drills must meet the following criteria: (1) during each calendar year, the appropriate local law enforcement agency shall contact the appropriate school administrator to request participation in a law enforcement drill and may actively participate on-site in a drill; and (2) upon completion of the law enforcement drill, the appropriate law enforcement official shall certify that the law enforcement drill was conducted. Schools may also conduct additional law enforcement drills.

Severe Weather and Shelter-In-Place Drill:
Schools must conduct a minimum of one severe weather and shelter-in-place drill to address and prepare students and school personnel for possible tornado incidents and may conduct additional severe weather and shelter-in-place drills to account for other incidents, including without limitation, earthquakes or hazardous material.

Information in this section comes, in part, from the Illinois State Board of Education's website at www.isbe.net. For additional information, see the Illinois State Board of Education's school emergency and crisis response plan template at: www.isbe.state.il.us/safety/guide.htm.

2.10 Sex Offenders at School
It is unlawful for a convicted child sex offender to be present at school or on school property, with very few exceptions. If the sex offender is a parent of a student in the building, the sex offender may come on school grounds in order to attend a conference with school officials related to his or her child's education, including participation in special education meetings. Other than these circumstances, a convicted child sex offender must obtain permission from the district superintendent or school board before coming on school property.

It is also illegal for a convicted child sex offender to be present within 100 feet of a school bus stop or 500 feet of school property.

<u>All convicted child sex offenders must check in and out of the school building with school officials whenever on school property and must remain directly supervised whenever in the vicinity of children under the age of 18.</u>

The law limiting child sex offenders from being present on school property also applies to students who are convicted child sex offenders. As such, schools must assure that students who fall into this category are properly supervised so as to assure the safety of all other students. This involves placing the student on what we call a "student sex offender management plan," which involves making sure that the student is adequately monitored while traveling to and from school, while at school and while at all school activities and events. Furthermore, this plan must also comply with State and Federal Student Records Acts make sure that the student's privacy is protected. For additional information on student records, see Chapter 4.

2.11 Animals on School Property

In order to assure student health and safety, many schools and districts prohibit animals on school property, except in the case of a service animal accompanying a student or other individual with a documented disability. In accordance with Federal Rules, only dogs are recognized as "service animals" under the Americans with Disabilities Act (ADA). Specifically, a service animal is defined as a dog that is individually trained to do work or perform tasks for a person with disabilities. Dogs whose sole function is to provide comfort or emotional support do not qualify as service animals under the ADA.

When it is not obvious what service an animal provides, only limited inquiries are allowed. School staff may only ask two questions:

1. Is the service animal required because of a disability?
2. What work or task has the dog been trained to perform?

School staff cannot ask about the person's disability, require medical documentation, require a special identification card or training documentation for the dog, or ask that the dog demonstrate its ability to perform the work or task. Allergies and fear of dogs are not valid reasons for denying access or refusing service to students, staff or members of the public who are using service animals.

FAQs

Must school districts comply with copyright laws?

Yes. Copyright law extends to all original works of authorship, including software programs, CD-ROM and web pages. Additionally, it is no longer required that an author place notice on the document or register it in order to receive all of the rights enumerated by the Federal Copyright Act. For additional information, see Section 2.7.

What is the Freedom of Information Act?

The Freedom of Information Act, commonly referred to as FOIA, is a State law that is aimed at giving the public access to government records. It is a means of providing oversight and assuring voters that governmental entities – including school districts – are complying with laws as well as internal policies and procedures. For additional information, see Section 2.8.

What types of evacuation drills are required each year and how many?

A minimum of one bus evacuation drill per building; three fire drills; one law enforcement drill (may be conducted without children present); and one severe weather and shelter-in-place drill. Other drills may be scheduled as determined by the district. For additional information, see Section 2.9.

What do the sirens mean?

Most systems use two siren tones. When they are activated, the sirens sound for a set amount of time, as determined by your community.
- Alert: A single tone signifying an emergency alert. This signal may be used for an emergency or disaster, including a severe storm, tornado warning (not a tornado watch), earthquake, chemical hazard/hazardous material incident, extreme winds or biological hazard.
- All Clear: Not used by all communities. Tune in to your local news agencies and listen for notification from city officials regarding the emergency.

What are the signs of a tornado?

Tornadoes vary greatly in their appearance and can occur with little or no warning. It is important to know the signs that a tornado could be imminent. Signs of a tornado include the following:
- A dark, often greenish sky
- A wall cloud, particularly if it is rotating
- Large hail, which is often produced by the same storms that produce tornadoes
- A loud roar, similar to the sound of a freight train
- Tornadoes may occur and be visible near the trailing edge of a thunderstorm
- Tornadoes may also be embedded in rain and not visible

What terms are used by the National Weather Service for winter storms?

- Wind Chill Advisory - dangerous wind chills of 15 below to 24 below zero are expected
- Wind Chill Warning - potentially life threatening wind chills of 25 below zero or colder are expected
- Frost Advisory - damaging frost is expected during the growing season
- Freeze Warning - below freezing temperatures are expected during the growing season
- Ice Storm Warning - dangerous accumulations of ice will occur and are expected to result in hazardous travel, extended power outages, and damage to trees
- Heavy Snow Warning - snow accumulations of six inches or greater, which will result in hazardous travel conditions
- Winter Weather Advisory - cold, ice and/or snow (two to five inches) are expected
- Winter Storm Watch - severe winter weather, such as heavy snow or ice, is possible within the next day or two
- Winter Storm Warning - severe ice and/or snow (six inches or more) have begun or are about to begin
- Blizzard Warning - heavy snow and strong winds will produce a blinding snow near zero visibility, deep drifts and life-threatening travel conditions

What terms are used by the National Weather Service in the event of flash floods?

- Flood/Flash Flood Watch - conditions are favorable for flooding in the next day or two. Flash floods occur very quickly, usually as a result of heavy rainfall in a short period of time
- Flood Warning - flooding is expected to threaten life and property a few hours after the onset of heavy rain, ice jams, reservoir releases or snowmelt. Flood warnings may be in effect for days or even weeks depending on weather and soil conditions, land topography, and river size
- Flash Flood Warning - rapidly rising water which poses an immediate threat to life and property within a few hours due to small stream or urban flooding and dam or levee failures. Quickly move to higher ground or stay away from flooded areas - especially in vehicles
- Flood Statement - ponding of water in urban areas or minor flooding of streams is occurring. Also used to convey supplemental information, updated observations, and impact information for Flood Warnings

Are Sex offenders allowed to be on school property?

It is unlawful for a convicted child sex offender to be present at school or school property, with very few exceptions. For additional information, see Section 2.10.

Are animals allowed on school property?

The answer depends on your school or district policy. For more information on service animals for persons with disabilities, see Section 2.11.

Checklists and Sample Forms

Sample forms available at www.edlawyer.org

Checklist 2-1: Valid Reasons to Deny a FOIA Request

- Test questions, scoring keys and other examination data used to administer an academic examination
- Information received by a primary or secondary school under its procedures for the evaluation of faculty members by their academic peers
- Information concerning a school's adjudication of student disciplinary cases, but only to the extent that disclosure would unavoidably reveal the identity of the student
- Course materials or research materials used by faculty members
- Interfere with active administrative enforcement proceedings conducted by the public body that is the recipient of the request
- Create a substantial likelihood that a person will be deprived of a fair trial or an impartial hearing
- Unavoidably disclose the identity of a confidential source, confidential information furnished only by the confidential source, or persons who file complaints with or provide information to administrative, investigative, law enforcement, or penal agencies
- Endanger the life or physical safety of any person
- Preliminary drafts, notes, recommendations, memoranda and other records in which opinions are expressed, or policies or actions are formulated
- Proposals and bids for any contract, grant, or agreement, including information which if it were disclosed would frustrate procurement or give an advantage to any person proposing to enter into a contractor agreement with the body, until an award or final selection is made
- Minutes of meetings of public bodies closed to the public as provided in the Open Meetings Act until the public body makes the minutes available to the public
- Communications between a public body and an attorney or auditor representing the public body that would not be subject to discovery in litigation, and materials prepared or compiled by or for a public body in anticipation of a criminal, civil or administrative proceeding upon the request of an attorney advising the public body, and materials prepared or compiled with respect to internal audits of public bodies
- Records relating to a public body's adjudication of employee grievances or disciplinary cases; however, this exemption shall not extend to the final outcome of cases in which discipline is imposed
- Records relating to collective negotiating matters between public bodies and their employees or representatives, except that any final contract or agreement shall be subject to inspection and copying
- Test questions, scoring keys, and other examination data used to determine the qualifications of an applicant for a license or employment

Freedom of Information Act, 5 ILCS 140/7

Checklist 2-2: Valid Reasons Allowing School Districts to Extend FOIA Deadline by Five Additional Days

- The requested records are stored in whole or in part at other locations than the office having charge of the requested records
- The request requires the collection of a substantial number of specified records
- The request is couched in categorical terms and requires an extensive search for the records responsive to it
- The requested records have not been located in the course of routine search and additional efforts are being made to locate them
- The requested records require examination and evaluation by personnel having the necessary competence and discretion to determine if they are exempt from disclosure
- The request for records cannot be complied with by the public body within the time limits prescribed without unduly burdening or interfering with the operations of the public body
- There is a need for consultation with another public body or among two or more components of a public body having a substantial interest in the determination or in the subject matter of the request

Freedom of Information Act, 5 ILCS 140/3

Illinois Law in the School Office   The School Office: First Line of Contact

Sample Form 2-1 – School Drill Documentation

SCHOOL DRILL DOCUMENTATION

DISTRICT NAME AND NUMBER	SCHOOL NAME	PRINCIPAL IN CHARGE

DRILL TYPE	INCIDENT TYPE	SIMULATED CONDITION	DATE	TIME
EVACUATION 1	FIRE			

Initials of Key School Participants and Backups | Evaluation of Drill Objectives (Check "S" for satisfactory or "I" for improvement(s) needed.)

Discovery	Leader	Monitor	Spokesperson	Recorder	Notification Effectiveness	Planned Response Understood	Movement to Safe Area	First Responder Communication	Accounting for Occupants
					☐S ☐I	☐S ☐I	☐S ☐I	☐S ☐I	☐S ☐I

Local Fire Official Present? ☐ Yes ☐ No Local Fire Official's Initials to certify that a school evacuation drill was conducted while present _____

DRILL TYPE	INCIDENT TYPE	SIMULATED CONDITION	DATE	TIME
EVACUATION 2	FIRE			

Initials of Key School Participants and Backups | Evaluation of Drill Objectives (Check "S" for satisfactory or "I" for improvement(s) needed.)

Discovery	Leader	Monitor	Spokesperson	Recorder	Notification Effectiveness	Planned Response Understood	Movement to Safe Area	First Responder Communication	Accounting for Occupants
					☐S ☐I	☐S ☐I	☐S ☐I	☐S ☐I	☐S ☐I

Local Fire Official Present? ☐ Yes ☐ No Local Fire Official's Initials to certify that a school evacuation drill was conducted while present _____

DRILL TYPE	INCIDENT TYPE	SIMULATED CONDITION	DATE	TIME
EVACUATION 3	FIRE			

Initials of Key School Participants and Backups | Evaluation of Drill Objectives (Check "S" for satisfactory or "I" for improvement(s) needed.)

Discovery	Leader	Monitor	Spokesperson	Recorder	Notification Effectiveness	Planned Response Understood	Movement to Safe Area	First Responder Communication	Accounting for Occupants
					☐S ☐I	☐S ☐I	☐S ☐I	☐S ☐I	☐S ☐I

Local Fire Official Present? ☐ Yes ☐ No Local Fire Official's Initials to certify that a school evacuation drill was conducted while present _____

DRILL TYPE	INCIDENT TYPE	SIMULATED CONDITION	DATE	TIME
BUS EVACUATION 1				

Initials of Key School Participants and Backups | Evaluation of Drill Objectives (Check "S" for satisfactory or "I" for improvement(s) needed.)

Discovery	Leader	Monitor	Spokesperson	Recorder	Notification Effectiveness	Planned Response Understood	Movement to Safe Area	First Responder Communication	Accounting for Occupants
					☐S ☐I	☐S ☐I	☐S ☐I	☐S ☐I	☐S ☐I

Drill accounted for in Curriculum? ☐ Yes ☐ No Curriculum includes instruction safe bus riding practices for all students? ☐ Yes ☐ No

DRILL TYPE	INCIDENT TYPE	SIMULATED CONDITION	DATE	TIME
SHELTER IN PLACE 1	TORNADO			

Initials of Key School Participants and Backups | Evaluation of Drill Objectives (Check "S" for satisfactory or "I" for improvement(s) needed.)

Discovery	Leader	Monitor	Spokesperson	Recorder	Notification Effectiveness	Planned Response Understood	Movement to Safe Area	First Responder Communication	Accounting for Occupants
					☐S ☐I	☐S ☐I	☐S ☐I	☐S ☐I	☐S ☐I

Local First Responder Present? ☐ Yes ☐ No Local First Responder's Initials to certify that a shelter-in-place drill was conducted while present _____

DRILL TYPE	INCIDENT TYPE	SIMULATED CONDITION	DATE	TIME
LAW ENFORCEMENT 1				

Initials of Key School Participants and Backups | Evaluation of Drill Objectives (Check "S" for satisfactory or "I" for improvement(s) needed.)

Discovery	Leader	Monitor	Spokesperson	Recorder	Notification Effectiveness	Planned Response Understood	Movement to Safe Area	First Responder Communication	Accounting for Occupants
					☐S ☐I	☐S ☐I	☐S ☐I	☐S ☐I	☐S ☐I

Local Law Enforcement Present? ☐ Yes ☐ No Local Law Enforcement's Initials to certify that a school lockdown drill was conducted while present _____

CC: Appropriate Regional Superintendent or OSFM if non-public school

ISBE 91-02 (9/11)   ISBE/OSFM Guidance - For Illinois School Use in Documenting the Completion of Minimum Drill Requirements III. D.

Illinois State Board of Education Form 91-02 (09/11)

References

105 ILCS 5/11-9.3. Presence within School Zone by Child Sex Offenders Prohibited. (Relevant text only)

Presence within school zone by child sex offenders prohibited; approaching, contacting, residing with, or communicating with a child within certain places by child sex offenders prohibited.

(a) It is unlawful for a child sex offender to knowingly be present in any school building, on real property comprising any school, or in any conveyance owned, leased, or contracted by a school to transport students to or from school or a school related activity when persons under the age of 18 are present in the building, on the grounds or in the conveyance, unless the offender is a parent or guardian of a student attending the school and the parent or guardian is: (i) attending a conference at the school with school personnel to discuss the progress of his or her child academically or socially, (ii) participating in child review conferences in which evaluation and placement decisions may be made with respect to his or her child regarding special education services, or (iii) attending conferences to discuss other student issues concerning his or her child such as retention and promotion and notifies the principal of the school of his or her presence at the school or unless the offender has permission to be present from the superintendent or the school board or in the case of a private school from the principal. In the case of a public school, if permission is granted, the superintendent or school board president must inform the principal of the school where the sex offender will be present. Notification includes the nature of the sex offender's visit and the hours in which the sex offender will be present in the school. The sex offender is responsible for notifying the principal's office when he or she arrives on school property and when he or she departs from school property. If the sex offender is to be present in the vicinity of children, the sex offender has the duty to remain under the direct supervision of a school official.

(a-5) It is unlawful for a child sex offender to knowingly be present within 100 feet of a site posted as a pick-up or discharge stop for a conveyance owned, leased, or contracted by a school to transport students to or from school or a school related activity when one or more persons under the age of 18 are present at the site.

(a-10) It is unlawful for a child sex offender to knowingly be present in any public park building or on real property comprising any public park when persons under the age of 18 are present in the building or on the grounds and to approach, contact, or communicate with a child under 18 years of age, unless the offender is a parent or guardian of a person under 18 years of age present in the building or on the grounds.

(b) It is unlawful for a child sex offender to knowingly loiter within 500 feet of a school building or real property comprising any school while persons under the age of 18 are present in the building or on the grounds, unless the offender is a parent or guardian of a student attending the school and the parent or guardian is: (i) attending a conference at the school with school personnel to discuss the progress of his or her child academically or socially, (ii) participating in child review conferences in which evaluation and placement decisions may be made with respect to his or her child regarding special education services, or (iii) attending conferences to discuss other student issues concerning his or her child such as retention and promotion and notifies the principal of the school of his or her presence at the school or has permission to be present from the superintendent or the school board or in the case of a private school from the principal. In the case of a public school, if permission is granted, the superintendent or school board president must inform the principal of the school where the sex offender will be present. Notification includes the nature of the sex offender's visit and the hours in which the sex offender will be present in the school. The sex offender is responsible for notifying the principal's office when he or she arrives on school property and when he or she departs from school property. If the sex offender is to be present in the vicinity of children, the sex offender has the duty to remain under the direct supervision of a school official.

(b-2) It is unlawful for a child sex offender to knowingly loiter on a public way within 500 feet of a public park building or real property comprising any public park while persons under the age of 18 are present in the building or on the grounds and to approach, contact, or communicate with a child under 18 years of age, unless the offender is a parent or guardian of a person under 18 years of age present in the building or on the grounds.

(b-5) It is unlawful for a child sex offender to knowingly reside within 500 feet of a school building or the real property comprising any school that persons under the age of 18 attend. Nothing in this subsection (b-5) prohibits a child sex offender from residing within 500 feet of a school building or the real property comprising any school that persons under 18 attend if the property is owned by the child sex offender and was purchased before the effective date of this amendatory Act of the 91st General Assembly.

(b-10) It is unlawful for a child sex offender to knowingly reside within 500 feet of a playground, child care institution, day care center, part day child care facility, day care home, group day care home, or a facility providing programs or services exclusively directed toward persons under 18 years of age. Nothing in this subsection (b-10) prohibits a child sex offender from residing within 500 feet of a playground or a facility providing programs or services exclusively directed toward persons under 18 years of age if the property is owned by the child sex offender and was purchased before July 7, 2000. Nothing in this subsection (b-10) prohibits a child sex offender from residing within 500 feet of a child care institution, day care center, or part day child care facility if the property is owned by the child sex offender and was purchased before June 26, 2006. Nothing in this subsection (b-10) prohibits a child sex offender from residing within 500 feet of a day care home or group day care home if the property is owned by the child sex offender and was purchased before August 14, 2008 (the effective date of Public Act 95-821).

(b-15) It is unlawful for a child sex offender to knowingly reside within 500 feet of the victim of the sex offense. Nothing in this subsection (b-15) prohibits a child sex offender from residing within 500 feet of the victim if the property in which the child sex offender resides is owned by the child sex offender and was purchased before August 22, 2002.

This subsection (b-15) does not apply if the victim of the sex offense is 21 years of age or older.

Chapter 3

Residency, Enrollment and Withdrawal

"For every complex problem, there is a solution that is simple, neat and wrong."
– H.L. Menchken

In This Chapter:

    3.1   Introduction
    3.2   Proof of Residency
    3.3   Other Enrollment Factors and Criteria
    3.4   Students Who Move During the School Year
    3.5   Homeless Students
    3.6   Foster Children
    3.7   Military Families
    3.8   Illegal Aliens
    3.9   Students Receiving Special Education Services
    3.10 Students Who Are Not Residents of the District
    3.11 The Tuition Option
    3.12 Truancy
    3.13 Withdrawal from School
    3.14 Special Circumstances Impacting Enrollment

FAQs
Checklists and Sample Forms
References

3.1 Introduction

Student residency is one of the most confusing and misunderstood areas of Illinois school law. The residency statute provides that a student is a resident of the school district where the person who has "legal custody" of the student lives. However, the definition of legal custodian in the residency statute does not necessarily mean the student's parent or guardian. For purposes of residency, legal custody means:

1. The student's natural or adoptive parent with whom the student lives; or
2. The person granted custody by a court order; or
3. A person given short-term guardianship by a court; or
4. An adult caregiver relative receiving public aid and with whom the student lives; or
5. Any adult who demonstrates and exercises responsibility for the student and provides the student with a set night-time residence.

Because the residency statute provides all of the above options, the legal custodian for residency purposes is really the person with whom the student lives and who is taking care of the student. The only exception is that a student cannot move in with an adult caregiver for the sole purpose of attending school in that district.

Consider the following example: Jim is a high school student whose parents live in School District A. However, Jim does not get along with his parents and lives with his girlfriend, Debbie, and her parents in School District B. Because Debbie's parents are caring for Jim and providing him with a fixed place to live, Debbie's parents have "legal custody" over Jim for school enrollment purposes. This means that Jim can go to school – tuition free – in School District B. The only exception would be if Jim moved in with Debbie and her parents only so that he could go to school in School District B, which is clearly not the case here.

It is critical to note, however, that the above definition of legal custody only applies for the purposes of enrollment. The student's actual parent or guardian (or the person who has actual custody of the student) is the one who the school must communicate with and who must make all medical and educational decisions on behalf of the student. Hence, in the above scenario, the school must still communicate with Jim's actual parent regarding all medical and educational decisions that impact Jim. Debbie's parents only have legal custody of Jim for the purpose of determining where he may go to school on a tuition free basis.

In a situation where a student is living with a person other than his or her parent or guardian, it is critical for the school district to continue to communicate with the student's parent or guardian. Alternatively, the parent or guardian may give the student's caregiver decision-making capabilities. This is often easier said than done, however, and we strongly recommend that you consult with your school principal in these cases to determine the sufficiency of such notice.

3.2 Proof of Residency

Schools and school districts may demand proof that a student lives within the boundaries of the school district. A determination of residency should generally be made before a student is enrolled in the school, as it is more difficult to remove a student from attendance for residency reasons after the student has been enrolled. Note, however, if a student is homeless the student must be admitted prior to questioning the student's residency.

In attempting to establish residency, a school or district may require documents such as a mortgage, rental agreement, power or electric bill or other reliable information that would indicate residence. A school or district must, however, allow parents some flexibility as to what documentation is required to prove residency. For example, a school or district could not require proof of home ownership, as not every resident owns their own home. Requiring proof of home ownership or a rental agreement would be more acceptable.

3.3 Other Enrollment Factors and Criteria

In addition to the residency requirement, there are other criteria that must be established when a student enrolls in school. Prior to enrollment, the student must present a student in good standing form indicating that the student is not currently subject to a suspension or expulsion from another school. Note that if the student is currently serving a suspension or expulsion from another school for drugs, alcohol or battery against a staff member, the student may not be enrolled in the new district until the term of the suspension or expulsion has expired. If the student is currently serving a suspension or expulsion from another school for any other reason, your school district's policy governs whether or not the student can be admitted. Some school districts have a policy honoring the suspension or expulsion of a student's prior school district.

Within 30 days of enrollment, the individual enrolling the student must provide the school with an original birth certificate or other reliable proof of the student's identity and an affidavit explaining why the birth certificate is not available. School officials must make a copy of the birth certificate for the student's record and return the original. If the individual enrolling the student fails to meet this requirement, the school must notify the Department of Children and Family Services (DCFS) or local police and also notify the person enrolling the child that he or she has 10 additional days to provide a birth certificate or other reliable proof of the child's identity. School officials must again notify DCFS or local police if this requirement is not met or the documents appear suspicious.

A student must also present up-to-date medical records, including proof of immunizations. If the student's medical records and immunizations are not up-to-date, the student must show proof of compliance by October 15, or an earlier date if required by the school district.

Lastly, upon enrollment, school officials should obtain a copy of a student's unofficial academic transcript and request from the student's last school district a full copy of the student's record. A student cannot be denied enrollment due to failure to present his or her student records.

3.4 Students Who Move During the School Year

According to the Illinois School Code, a student who moves out of the school district at any time during the school year may continue to attend school in the district – tuition free – for the remainder of the school year. Beyond the end of the school year, the student must attend school in the new school district where the student lives or tuition into the former school district.

3.5 Homeless Students

Under State and Federal law, a student is homeless if the student lacks a fixed nighttime abode or, put simply, does not have a permanent place to live. A student is also considered homeless if the student's permanent residence is a shelter or other place not intended as a place for people to live. The definition of homeless also includes individuals sharing a residence due to loss of housing or economic hardship or living in a hotel, trailer park or campgrounds due to a lack of alternative adequate accommodations.

Students who are homeless may generally attend school on a tuition free basis in one of three places:
1. The school in which he or she was enrolled when permanently housed (also known as the "school of origin");
2. The school in which he or she was last enrolled; or
3. Any public school that non-homeless students who live in the attendance area are eligible to attend.

A homeless student may not be denied enrollment in a school district due to his or her failure to produce normally required enrollment documents, such as academic records, medical records and proof of residency.

3.6 Foster Children

Foster children who are five or older by September 1 are required by the Department of Children and Family Services to attend school. Foster children generally attend the school where their foster parents reside, although DCFS is ultimately responsible for determining the appropriate school for a foster child.

3.7 Military Families

If a student's change of residence is due to the military service obligation of a person who has legal custody of the student, then, upon the written request of the person having legal custody of the student, the residence of the student is deemed for all purposes relating to enrollment (including tuition, fees and costs), for the duration of the custodian's military service obligation, to be the same as the residence of the student immediately before the change of residence caused by the military service obligation. A school district is not responsible for providing transportation for the student in this situation.

3.8 Illegal Aliens

The immigration status of parents and children has no bearing on the right of children to enroll in school. As such, school districts may not question a child's immigration status as part of the enrollment process. Furthermore, a school district may not, as part of a residency inquiry, require that parents or adult caretakers provide either a Visa, "Green Card," Illinois driver's license, a state identification card or other documents that require a Social Security number.

3.9 Students Receiving Special Education Services

Residency of students receiving special education services is a different and more complicated process than with other students. The resident district is the school district in which the parent or guardian of the student resides when:

1. The parent has legal guardianship of the student and resides within Illinois;
2. An individual guardian has been appointed by the courts and resides within Illinois;
3. An Illinois public agency has legal guardianship and the student resides either in the home of the parent or within the same district as the parent; or
4. An Illinois court orders a residential placement but the parents retain any legal rights or guardianship and have not been subject to a termination of parental rights order.

In cases of divorced or separated parents, when only one parent has legal guardianship or custody, the district in which the parent having legal guardianship or custody resides is the resident district. When both parents retain legal guardianship or custody, the resident district is the district in which either parent who provides the student's primary regular fixed nighttime abode resides; provided that the election of resident district may be made only one time per school year.

The resident district is the school district in which the student resides when:
1. The parent has legal guardianship but the location of the parent is unknown;
2. An individual guardian has been appointed but the location of the guardian is unknown;
3. The student is 18 years of age or older and no legal guardian has been appointed;
4. The student is legally an emancipated minor; or
5. An Illinois public agency has legal guardianship and such agency or any court in this State has placed the student residentially outside of the school district in which the parent lives.

3.10 Students Who Are Not Residents of the District

If a school district determines that a student who is attending school in the district on a tuition free basis is a nonresident of the district for whom tuition is required to be charged, the district shall notify the person who enrolled the pupil of the amount of the tuition that is due for the nonresident student's attendance in the district's schools. The notice shall be given by certified mail, return receipt requested.

Within 10 days after receipt of the notice, the person who enrolled the student may request a hearing to review the determination of the school district. The request shall be sent by certified mail, return receipt requested, to the district superintendent. Within 10 days after receipt of the request, the board shall notify, by certified mail, return receipt requested, the person requesting the hearing of the time and place of the hearing, which shall be held not less than 10 or more than 20 days after the notice of hearing is given.

The board or a hearing officer designated by the board shall conduct the hearing. The board and the person who enrolled the pupil may be represented at the hearing by representatives of their choice. At the hearing, the person who enrolled the student has the burden of showing that he or she is actually a resident of the district. The school board or hearing officer must, within 15 days after the conclusion of the hearing, decide whether or not the pupil is a resident of the district and, if not, the amount of any tuition required. The school board shall send a copy of its decision to the person who enrolled the student. The decision of the school board is final.

If a student is determined to be a nonresident of the district for whom tuition is required to be charged, the board shall refuse to permit the student to continue attending the school unless the required tuition is paid.

A person who knowingly enrolls or attempts to enroll on a tuition free basis a student known by that person to be a non-resident of the district is potentially be guilty of a Class C misdemeanor.

3.11 The Tuition Option

School districts may, by policy, permit nonresident students to attend school in the district on a tuition basis. School districts must charge tuition of between 100 % and 110 % of costs for students who are not residents of the district and who do not fit into one of the exceptions discussed in this chapter.

3.12 Truancy

According to the Illinois School Code, a student is "excused" from school for one of the following reasons: illness, observation of a religious holiday, death in the immediate family, family emergency, other situations beyond control of the student as determined by the local board of education, or other circumstances which cause reasonable concern to the parent for the safety or health of the student. In all other situations, the student is considered to be unexcused and truant.

3.13 Withdrawal from School

According to State law, a child must attend school until the age of 17. When a child reaches the age of 17, the child's parent or guardian can permanently withdraw the child from school. However, when a student reaches 18 years of age, and is therefore an adult, the student can withdraw himself of herself from school.

When a child withdraws from school in order to attend school in another district, the sending school must, within 10 days, forward to the new school the student's unofficial academic transcript. If the child is transferring to another school in Illinois, the sending school must also forward to the new school a completed "good standing form." The remainder of the student's record must be sent to the new school within 10 days of the new school making a request. For more information, see Checklist 3-1.

3.14 Special Circumstances Impacting Enrollment

A school district is required to deny enrollment to a high school student who is 19 years of age or older and who has dropped out of school and could not, because of age and lack of credits, attend classes during the normal school year and graduate before his or her twenty-first birthday. A school district may, however, enroll these students in a graduate incentive program. This provision does not apply to students receiving special education services.

Additionally, under certain circumstances, a school district may deny enrollment to a student 17 years of age or older for one semester for failure to meet minimum academic standards.

A school district that denies a student reenrollment or enrollment in accordance with the above circumstances must afford the student a full due process hearing.

FAQs

At what age must students attend school?

Under the Illinois compulsory education statute, students between the ages of 7 and 17 must attend school, with extremely limited exceptions.

What documents should a school district request when a child first enrolls?

Enrollment documents include proof of residency, a student in good standing form (or proof the student is not currently subject to a suspension or expulsion from another school), medical records and a birth certificate. See Sections 3.2 and 3.3 and Checklist 3-1 for additional information.

At what age may a student first attend Kindergarten?

A child who will be five on or before September 1 of the school year may attend school. A school district may allow younger children to attend school (on a case by case determination) based on each child's readiness. Kindergarten attendance is optional based on the decision of the parent or guardian.

Where does a student attend school on a tuition free basis?

A student attends school tuition free in the legal custodian's school district. For the purposes of residency, the legal custodian is:

1. The student's natural or adoptive parent with whom the student lives; or
2. The person granted custody by a court order; or
3. A person given short-term guardianship by a court; or
4. An adult caregiver relative receiving public aid and with whom the student lives; or
5. Any adult who demonstrates and exercises responsibility for the student and provides the student with a set night-time residence.

See Section 3.1 for additional information.

Can a school require a student to prove residency?

Yes. In attempting to establish residency, a school or district may request documents such as a mortgage, rental agreement, power or electric bill or other reliable information that would indicate residence. See Section 3.2 for additional information.

Can a student attend school in the district if the student moves during the school year?

A student who moves out of the school district at any time during the school year may continue to attend school at the school district – tuition free – for the remainder of the school year. See Section 3.4 for additional information.

Where can a homeless student attend school on a tuition free basis?

Students who are homeless may generally attend school on a tuition free basis in one of three places:

1. The school in which he or she was enrolled when permanently housed (also known as the "school of origin");
2. The school in which he or she was last enrolled; or
3. Any public school that non-homeless students who live in the attendance area are eligible to attend.

See Section 3.5 for additional information.

Where do students who are in foster care attend school?

Foster children generally attend the school where their foster parents reside, although DCFS is ultimately responsible for determining the appropriate school for a foster child.

Are students required to be U.S. citizens in order to attend school?

The immigration status of a parent or child has no bearing on the right of children in school. As such, school districts may not question a child's immigration status as part of the enrollment process. See Section 3.8 for additional information.

What happens if a school district discovers that a student is not a resident of the school district?

In these cases, the school district must provide notice to the legal custodian indicating that the school district believes that the student is not properly a resident of the district. The legal custodian may request a hearing before the school board, withdraw the student or opt to pay tuition. See Sections 3.10 and 3.11 for additional information.

When is a student considered truant?

According to the Illinois School Code, a student is "excused" from school for one of the following reasons: illness, observation of a religious holiday, death in the immediate family, family emergency, other situations beyond control of the student as determined by the local board of education, and/or other circumstances which cause reasonable concern to the parent for the safety or health of the student. In all other situations, the student is considered to be unexcused and truant.

Can a school district require a parent to officially withdraw a student prior to homeschooling the student?

No. In Illinois, a parent need only tell the school orally that the parent is going to homeschool the child. School officials may request that the parent complete a homeschool registration form, but this is optional on the part of the parent.

Is an 18 year old student entitled to make his or her own decisions?

When a student reaches 18 years of age, the student is legally an adult and can request to make all of his or her own decisions regarding school. Furthermore, an 18 year old student can request that school officials no longer communicate with the student's parent or guardian regarding the student's education.

Checklists and Sample Forms

Sample forms available at www.edlawyer.org

Checklist 3-1: Recordkeeping Requirements When Students Enroll in or Withdraw from School
(Included are the recordkeeping requirements when a student enrolls in school or withdraws from school.)

Recordkeeping Responsibilities of the Sending School	Recordkeeping Responsibilities of the Receiving School
• Review the student's record and eliminate or correct all out-of-date, misleading, inaccurate, unnecessary or irreverent information • Notify parents of the record destruction schedule • Send a transcript of the student's grades • Send the remainder of the student's record within 10 days of a request • Note: Do not forward original records, they must be maintained by your school district. Send copies of records only • Prepare a Student in Good Standing Form if the student is transferring to an Illinois public school	• Check proof of residency • Make sure the student has proper medical immunization • Review the Student in Good Standing Form if the student comes from another Illinois public school • If a student is transferring from an out of state school, require the student's parents or guardian to certify in writing that the student is not currently subject to a suspension or expulsion at the school the student is transferring from • Request a birth certificate or other reliable proof of identity to assure that the child has not been kidnapped or is not a missing child • Request records from the prior school, including the IEP if applicable

Residency, Enrollment and Withdrawal Illinois Law in the School Office

Sample Form 3-1: Affidavit of Enrollment and Residency

ILLINOIS STATE BOARD OF EDUCATION

AFFIDAVIT OF ENROLLMENT AND RESIDENCY

This affidavit form may be used if you are an adult who has assumed responsibility for a pupil and provide the pupil with a fixed, night-time abode, **for reasons other than access to the educational programs of the school district**.

This form should *not* be used, however, if you are the natural or adoptive parent of the pupil, have been granted court-ordered custody or guardianship, or are receiving public aid on behalf of the pupil. For these situations, you are only required to provide documentation (such as a birth certificate or court order), without the need of an affidavit like this one.

This form is also *not* required for pupils who are sharing the housing of others due to lack of housing, economic hardship, or similar reason, or are otherwise homeless as defined in state and federal law. **Homeless pupils must be enrolled immediately.**

If you have **any** questions about residency, including homelessness, please contact the Illinois State Board of Education's Educator and School Development Division at (217) 782-2948.

I, _____, reside at _____,
 Name of Adult *Address*
which is located within the boundaries of _____.
 School District

Provide the appropriate information and check each of the following:

☐ I am at least 18 years of age.

☐ I have provided proof in the form(s) of _____
 Proof of Residency
_____
that I am a resident of _____.
 School District

☐ I have assumed and exercise responsibility for _____.
 Name of Pupil

☐ I provide a fixed, night-time abode for _____.
 Name of Pupil

☐ _____ is not living with me for the purpose of having access to the educational programs
 Name of Pupil
of the school district.

☐ I understand that knowingly or willfully providing false information to a school district regarding the residency of a pupil for the purpose of enabling that pupil to attend any school in that district without the payment of nonresident tuition is a Class C misdemeanor.

☐ I understand that knowingly enrolling or attempting to enroll a pupil in the school of a school district of a tuition free basis when I know that pupil to be nonresident of the school district, unless the nonresident pupil has a lawful right to attend, is a Class C misdemeanor.

_____ _____ _____
 Date *Signature of Adult* *Adult (Print Name)*

_____ _____ _____
 Date *School District Employee (Signature)* *School District Employee (Print Name)*

ISBE 85-51 (8/09)

Illinois State Board of Education Form 85-51 (8/09)

Illinois Law in the School Office   Residency, Enrollment and Withdrawal

Sample Form 3-2: Student Transfer Form

ILLINOIS STATE BOARD OF EDUCATION
Educator and School Development Division
100 North First Street, E-310
Springfield, Illinois 62777-0001

STUDENT IDENTIFICATION NUMBER (9-digits)

STUDENT TRANSFER FORM

In accordance with Section 2-3.13a of the School Code, all public school districts are to provide this form to any student who is moving out of the school district to verify whether or not the student is "in good standing" and, whether or not their medical records are up-to-date and complete as defined in Section 2-3.13a. "In good standing" means that the student is not being disciplined by an out-of-school suspension or expulsion, and is entitled to attend classes, as of the date of this form. No public school district is required to admit a new student unless they can produce this form from the student's previous Illinois public school district. **This form is not to be returned to the Illinois State Board of Education. It is to be sent directly to the student's new school they will be attending.**

NAME OF STUDENT (Last, First, Middle)	BIRTHDATE (Month, Day, Year)	GENDER ☐ Male ☐ Female	GRADE LEVEL

ADDRESS OF STUDENT (Street, City, State, Zip Code)

NAME OF PARENT OR GUARDIAN	PARENT/GUARDIAN TELEPHONE (Include Area Code)
	Home Work

ADDRESS OF PARENT OR GUARDIAN (Street, City, State, Zip Code)

DISTRICT NAME AND NUMBER TRANSFERRING TO	NEW DISTRICT ADDRESS (City, State, Zip Code)

NAME OF SCHOOL STUDENT WILL BE TRANSFERRING TO	NAME OF PRINCIPAL AT NEW SCHOOL

Please check (✓) the appropriate box.

☐ I hereby attest that the above student is "in good standing" and that all medical records for the above student are up-to-date and complete as of the date of this form.

☐ The above student's medical records are **not** up-to-date and complete as documented in the student's permanent records.

☐ I hereby attest that the above student is **not** "in good standing" due to a current suspension and/or expulsion from _____ until _____; but is entitled to transfer in accordance with Section 2-3.13a (105 ILCS 5/2-3.13a), unless the receiving district has, pursuant to Section 2-3.13a, adopted a policy providing that if a student is suspended or expelled for any reason from any public or private school in this or any other state, the student must complete the entire term of the suspension or expulsion before being admitted into the school district. This policy may allow placement of the student in an alternative school program established under Article 13A of this Code, if available, for the remainder of the suspension or expulsion.

☐ I hereby attest that the above student is **not** "in good standing" due to a current suspension and/or expulsion from _____ until _____ and is **not** eligible for transfer for knowingly possessing in a school building or on school grounds a weapon as defined in the Gun Free Schools Act (20 U.S.C. 8921 et seq.); for knowingly possessing, selling, or delivering in a school building or on school grounds a controlled substance or cannabis; or for battering a staff member of the school.

NAME OF PRINCIPAL	SCHOOL PHONE	COUNTY

DISTRICT NAME AND NUMBER	DISTRICT ADDRESS (City, State, Zip Code)

_____   _____
Date   Signature of Principal

ISBE 33-78 (8/11)   **THIS FORM IS TO BE SENT DIRECTLY TO THE STUDENT'S NEW SCHOOL THEY WILL BE ATTENDING.**

Illinois State Board of Education Form 33-78 (8/11)

Residency, Enrollment and Withdrawal

Illinois Law in the School Office

Sample Form 3-3: Homeschool Registration Form

Illinois State Board of Education
Data Analysis and Progress Reporting
100 North First Street, S-284
Springfield, Illinois 62777-0001
Telephone #: 217/782-3950   Fax #: 217/524-7784

Home Schooling Registration
School Year Beginning in Fall _____ **(provide year)**

Directions: Please complete all areas of this form and return it to the Illinois State Board of Education at the address above. This form is electronically fillable or you may print a copy and complete it by hand—**PLEASE PRINT**.

PLEASE REMEMBER TO REGISTER EVERY SEPTEMBER.
Registration with the Illinois State Board of Education and/or your Regional Office of Education is voluntary.

NAME(S) OF PARENT(S) OR GUARDIAN(S)		COUNTY	
ADDRESS (Street, City, State, Zip Code)	TELEPHONE (Include Area Code)	FAX (Include Area Code)	
	E-MAIL		

Provide the full name of each child being taught and information for the current school year:

NAME	GRADE	GENDER MALE	GENDER FEMALE	DATE OF BIRTH (mm/dd/yyyy)
		☐	☐	___/___/___
		☐	☐	___/___/___
		☐	☐	___/___/___
		☐	☐	___/___/___
		☐	☐	___/___/___

Provide information on the last public or nonpublic school attended (if applicable):

CHILD	SCHOOL NAME	PUBLIC/NONPUBLIC (Check only one)		DATES OF ATTENDANCE (mm/dd/yyyy)
		☐	☐	___/___/___
		☐	☐	___/___/___
		☐	☐	___/___/___
		☐	☐	___/___/___
		☐	☐	___/___/___

Provide the name of the curriculum to be used: _____

Education areas being taught (check all that apply):
(Section 26-1 of the School Code states that areas of education must be taught in the English language)

☐ Language Arts   ☐ Mathematics   ☐ Biological and Physical Sciences

☐ Social Sciences   ☐ Fine Arts   ☐ Physical Development and Health

Other (please specify) _____

_____   _____
Signature of Parent/Guardian   Date (mm/dd/yyyy)

ISBE 87-02 (6/10)

Illinois State Board of Education Form 87-02 (6/10)

Sample Form 3-4: Homeless Student Enrollment / Withdrawal

ILLINOIS STATE BOARD OF EDUCATION
Curriculum and Instruction Division
100 North First Street, C-215
Springfield, Illinois 62777-0001

MCKINNEY-VENTO HOMELESS EDUCATION
SHELTERED HOMELESS/HOMELESS DOUBLED-UP STUDENT ENROLLMENT/ WITHDRAWAL

DISTRICT NAME AND NUMBER

PART I

Directions: Please complete Part I when initiating a request for service and fax to the school district.

DATE	PERSON REQUESTING ASSISTANCE	STUDENT NAME	DATE OF BIRTH	GRADE
TELEPHONE (Include Area Code)	FAX (Include Area Code)	PARENT/GUARDIAN NAME		
SCHOOL/SHELTER/AGENCY		SCHOOL/SHELTER/AGENCY ADDRESS (Street, City, State, Zip)		
TELEPHONE (Include Area Code)	FAX (Include Area Code)			

CHECK ONE
☐ RESIDENT ☐ OTHER _____

NATURE OF REQUEST
☐ ENROLLMENT ☐ TRANSPORTATION ☐ OTHER _____

IS STUDENT RECEIVING SPECIAL EDUCATION SERVICES?
☐ YES ☐ NO

NAME OF SCHOOL WHERE STUDENT LAST ATTENDED

SCHOOL OF ORIGIN

ADDITIONAL INFORMATION REGARDING STUDENT/FAMILY

DISTRICT NAME AND NUMBER

PART II

Directions: Part II is to be completed by the school staff liaison upon student's withdrawal.

DATE OF WITHDRAWAL

Name of Individual completing form (please print)   Signature   Date

Central Office Comments/Outcomes:

Please submit this form to your Area Homeless Liaison.
If you are not sure who your Area Homeless Liaison is please refer to the Area Homeless Liaison Breakdown Map.
http://www.isbe.net/homeless/pdf/mkv_liaison_map.pdf

ISBE 83-04D (5/11)

Illinois State Board of Education Form 83-04D (5/11)

Sample Form 3-5: Evidence of Non-Parent's Custody, Control, and Responsibility of a Student

This form establishes a child's residency in the School District when the child is not living with a natural or adoptive parent.) It must be completed by the individual who has assumed custody. Read Important Warning and submit this form with your signature to the Building Principal.

(Please print)

_____   _____
Student's name   District attendance building

_____   _____
Name of individual completing this form   Relationship to child

Please check all applicable boxes:
- ❏ The child lives with me at my residence address, as stated below, and is not living with me solely for the purpose of attending the District's school.
- ❏ I have assumed and exercise full legal responsibility for and control of the child regarding daily educational and medical decisions, including responsibility for:
  - ❏ medical decisions and costs   ❏ food and clothing
  - ❏ discipline and restitution for vandalism or other crimes ❏ school fees (books, bus, etc.)

At my residence the child regularly: *(Please explain any unchecked boxes)*
- ❏ Eats meals _____
- ❏ Sleeps _____
- ❏ Spends weekends and summers _____

Important Warning: The School District reserves the right to evaluate the evidence presented. Completing this form does not guarantee admission. If a student is determined to be a nonresident of the District for whom tuition must be charged, the persons enrolling the student are liable for non-resident tuition from the date the student began attending a District school as a non-resident.

A person who knowingly enrolls or attempts to enroll in this School District on a tuition-free basis a student known by that person to be a nonresident of the District is guilty of a Class C misdemeanor, except in very limited situations as defined in State law (105 ILCS 5/10-20.12b(e).

A person who knowingly or willfully presents to the School District any false information regarding a student's residency to enable that student to attend any school in the District without the payment of a nonresident tuition charge is guilty of a Class C misdemeanor (105 ILCS 5/10-20.12b(f).

_____   _____
Date   Signature of individual completing this form

_____   _____
Telephone   Address

Optional: To be completed by the natural or adoptive parent(s), if one is available.

Please check all applicable boxes:

☐ I am the natural or adoptive parent of the child.
☐ I have willingly transferred full custody and control of, as well as responsibility for this child to:

_____

☐ The transfer of custody is not solely for the purpose of attending the District's schools.

_____ _____
Date   Signature of individual completing this form

_____ _____
Telephone   Address

Used with Permission from Illinois Association of School Boards, PRESS Form7:60-AP2, E3 (02/09)

References

105 ILCS 5/10-20.12b. Residency; payment of tuition; hearing; criminal penalty.
(a) For purposes of this Section:
   (1) The residence of a person who has legal custody of a pupil is deemed to be the residence of the pupil.
   (2) "Legal custody" means one of the following:
      (i) Custody exercised by a natural or adoptive parent with whom the pupil resides.
      (ii) Custody granted by order of a court of competent jurisdiction to a person with whom the pupil resides for reasons other than to have access to the educational programs of the district.
      (iii) Custody exercised under a statutory short-term guardianship, provided that within 60 days of the pupil's enrollment a court order is entered that establishes a permanent guardianship and grants custody to a person with whom the pupil resides for reasons other than to have access to the educational programs of the district.
      (iv) Custody exercised by an adult caretaker relative who is receiving aid under the Illinois Public Aid Code for the pupil who resides with that adult caretaker relative for purposes other than to have access to the educational programs of the district.
      (v) Custody exercised by an adult who demonstrates that, in fact, he or she has assumed and exercises legal responsibility for the pupil and provides the pupil with a regular fixed night-time abode for purposes other than to have access to the educational programs of the district.

(a-5) If a pupil's change of residence is due to the military service obligation of a person who has legal custody of the pupil, then, upon the written request of the person having legal custody of the pupil, the residence of the pupil is deemed for all purposes relating to enrollment (including tuition, fees, and costs), for the duration of the custodian's military service obligation, to be the same as the residence of the pupil immediately before the change of residence caused by the military service obligation. A school district is not responsible for providing transportation to or from school for a pupil whose residence is determined under this subsection (a-5). School districts shall facilitate re-enrollment when necessary to comply with this subsection (a-5).

(b) Except as otherwise provided under Section 10-22.5a, only resident pupils of a school district may attend the schools of the district without payment of the tuition required to be charged under Section 10-20.12a. However, children for whom the Guardianship Administrator of the Department of Children and Family Services has been appointed temporary custodian or guardian of the person of a child shall not be charged tuition as a nonresident pupil if the child was placed by the Department of Children and Family Services with a foster parent or placed in another type of child care facility and the foster parent or child care facility is located in a school district other than the child's former school district and it is determined by the Department of Children and Family

Services to be in the child's best interest to maintain attendance at his or her former school district.

(c) The provisions of this subsection do not apply in school districts having a population of 500,000 or more. If a school board in a school district with a population of less than 500,000 determines that a pupil who is attending school in the district on a tuition free basis is a nonresident of the district for whom tuition is required to be charged under Section 10-20.12a, the board shall notify the person who enrolled the pupil of the amount of the tuition charged under Section 10-20.12a that is due to the district for the nonresident pupil's attendance in the district's schools. The notice shall be given by certified mail, return receipt requested. Within 10 days after receipt of the notice, the person who enrolled the pupil may request a hearing to review the determination of the school board. The request shall be sent by certified mail, return receipt requested, to the district superintendent. Within 10 days after receipt of the request, the board shall notify, by certified mail, return receipt requested, the person requesting the hearing of the time and place of the hearing, which shall be held not less than 10 nor more than 20 days after the notice of hearing is given. The board or a hearing officer designated by the board shall conduct the hearing. The board and the person who enrolled the pupil may be represented at the hearing by representatives of their choice. At the hearing, the person who enrolled the pupil shall have the burden of going forward with the evidence concerning the pupil's residency. If the hearing is conducted by a hearing officer, the hearing officer, within 5 days after the conclusion of the hearing, shall send a written report of his or her findings by certified mail, return receipt requested, to the school board and to the person who enrolled the pupil. The person who enrolled the pupil may, within 5 days after receiving the findings, file written objections to the findings with the school board by sending the objections by certified mail, return receipt requested, addressed to the district superintendent. Whether the hearing is conducted by the school board or a hearing officer, the school board shall, within 15 days after the conclusion of the hearing, decide whether or not the pupil is a resident of the district and the amount of any tuition required to be charged under Section 10-20.12a as a result of the pupil's attendance in the schools of the district. The school board shall send a copy of its decision to the person who enrolled the pupil, and the decision of the school board shall be final.

(c-5) The provisions of this subsection apply only in school districts having a population of 500,000 or more. If the board of education of a school district with a population of 500,000 or more determines that a pupil who is attending school in the district on a tuition free basis is a nonresident of the district for whom tuition is required to be charged under Section 10-20.12a, the board shall notify the person who enrolled the pupil of the amount of the tuition charged under Section 10-20.12a that is due to the district for the nonresident pupil's attendance in the district's schools. The notice shall be given by certified mail, return receipt requested. Within 10 days after receipt of the notice, the person who enrolled the pupil may request a hearing to review the determination of the school board. The request shall be sent by certified mail, return receipt requested, to the district superintendent. Within 30 days after receipt of the request, the board shall notify, by certified mail, return receipt requested, the person requesting the hearing of the time and place of the hearing, which shall be held not less than 10 nor more than 30 days after the notice of hearing is given. The board or a hearing officer designated by the board shall conduct the hearing. The board and the person who enrolled the pupil may each be represented at the hearing by a representative of their choice. At the hearing, the person who enrolled the pupil shall have the burden of going forward with the evidence concerning the pupil's residency. If the hearing is conducted by a hearing officer, the hearing officer, within 20 days after the conclusion of the hearing, shall serve a written report of his or her findings by personal service or by certified mail, return receipt requested, to the school board and to the person who enrolled the pupil. The person who enrolled the pupil may, within 10 days after receiving the findings, file written objections to the findings with the board of education by sending the objections by certified mail, return receipt requested, addressed to the general superintendent of schools. If the hearing is conducted by the board of education, the board shall, within 45 days after the conclusion of the hearing, decide whether or not the pupil is a resident of the district and the amount of any tuition required to be charged under Section 10-20.12a as a result of the pupil's attendance in the schools of the district. If the hearing is conducted by a hearing officer, the board of education shall, within 45 days after the receipt of the hearing officer's findings, decide whether or not the pupil is a resident of the district and the amount of any tuition required to be charged under Section 10-20.12a as a result of the pupil's attendance in the schools of the district. The board of education shall send, by certified mail, return receipt requested, a copy of its decision to the person who enrolled the pupil, and the decision of the board shall be final.

(d) If a hearing is requested under subsection (c) or (c-5) to review the determination of the school board or board of education that a nonresident pupil is attending the schools of the district without payment of the tuition required to be charged under Section 10-20.12a, the pupil may, at the request of a person who enrolled the pupil, continue attendance at the schools of the district pending a final decision of the board following the hearing. However, attendance of that pupil in the schools of the district as authorized by this subsection (d) shall not relieve any person who enrolled the pupil of the obligation to pay the tuition charged for that attendance under Section 10-20.12a if the final decision of the board is that the pupil is a nonresident of the district. If a pupil is determined to be a nonresident of the district for whom tuition is required to be charged pursuant to this Section, the board shall refuse to permit the pupil to continue attending the schools of the district unless the required tuition is paid for the pupil.

(e) Except for a pupil referred to in subsection (b) of Section 10-22.5a, a pupil referred to in Section 10-20.12a, or a pupil referred to in subsection (b) of this Section, a person who knowingly enrolls or attempts to enroll in the schools of a school district on a tuition free basis a pupil known by that person to be a nonresident of the district shall be guilty of a Class C misdemeanor.

(f) A person who knowingly or willfully presents to any school district any false information regarding the residency of a pupil for the purpose of enabling that pupil to attend any school in that district without the payment of a nonresident tuition charge shall be guilty of a Class C misdemeanor.

(g) The provisions of this Section are subject to the provisions of the Education for Homeless Children Act. Nothing in this Section shall be construed to apply to or require the payment of tuition by a parent or guardian of a "homeless child" (as that term is defined in Section 1-5 of the Education for Homeless Children Act) in connection with or as a result of the homeless child's continued education or enrollment in a school that is chosen in accordance with any of the options provided in Section 1-10 of that Act.

105 ILCS 5/14-1.11. Resident district; parent; legal guardian.

The resident district is the school district in which the parent or guardian, or both parent and guardian, of the student reside when:

(1) the parent has legal guardianship of the student and resides within Illinois; or

(2) an individual guardian has been appointed by the courts and resides within Illinois; or

(3) an Illinois public agency has legal guardianship and the student resides either in the home of the parent or within the same district as the parent; or

(4) an Illinois court orders a residential placement but the parents retain any legal rights or guardianship and have not been subject to a termination of parental rights order.

In cases of divorced or separated parents, when only one parent has legal guardianship or custody, the district in which the parent having legal guardianship or custody resides is the resident district. When both parents retain legal guardianship or custody, the resident district is the district in which either parent who provides the student's primary regular fixed nighttime abode resides; provided, that the election of resident district may be made only one time per school year.

When the parent has legal guardianship and lives outside of the State of Illinois, or when the individual legal guardian other than the natural parent lives outside the State of Illinois, the parent, legal guardian, or other placing agent is responsible for making arrangements to pay the Illinois school district serving the child for the educational services provided. Those service costs shall be determined in accordance with Section 14-7.01.

105 ILCS 5/15-1.11a Resident district; student

The resident district is the school district in which the student resides when:

(1) the parent has legal guardianship but the location of the parent is unknown; or

(2) an individual guardian has been appointed but the location of the guardian is unknown; or

(3) the student is 18 years of age or older and no legal guardian has been appointed; or

(4) the student is legally an emancipated minor; or

(5) an Illinois public agency has legal guardianship and such agency or any court in this State has placed the student residentially outside of the school district in which the parent lives.

In cases where an Illinois public agency has legal guardianship and has placed the student residentially outside of Illinois, the last school district that provided at least 45 days of educational service to the student shall continue to be the district of residence until the student is no longer under guardianship of an Illinois public agency or until the student is returned to Illinois.

The resident district of a homeless student is the Illinois district in which the student enrolls for educational services. Homeless students include individuals as defined in the Stewart B. McKinney Homeless Assistance Act.

105 ILCS 5/2-3.13a. School Records; Transferring Students.

(a) The State Board of Education shall establish and implement rules requiring all of the public schools and all private or nonpublic elementary and secondary schools located in this State, whenever any such school has a student who is transferring to any other public elementary or secondary school located in this or in any other state, to forward within 10 days of notice of the student's transfer an unofficial record of that student's grades to the school to which such student is transferring. Each public school at the same time also shall forward to the school to which the student is transferring the remainder of the student's school student records as required by the Illinois School Student Records Act. In addition, if a student is transferring from a public school, whether located in this or any other state, from which the student has been suspended or expelled for knowingly possessing in a school building or on school grounds a weapon as defined in the Gun Free Schools Act), for knowingly possessing, selling, or delivering in a school building or on school grounds a controlled substance or cannabis, or for battering a staff member of the school, and if the period of suspension or expulsion has not expired at the time the student attempts to transfer into another public school in the same or any other school district: (i) any school student records required to be transferred shall include the date and duration of the period of suspension or expulsion; and (ii) with the exception of transfers into the Department of Juvenile Justice school district, the student shall not be permitted to attend class in the public school into which he or she is transferring until the student has served the entire period of the suspension or expulsion imposed by the school from which the student is transferring, provided that the school board may approve the placement of the student in an alternative school program established under Article 13A of this Code. A school district may adopt a policy providing that if a student is suspended or expelled for any reason from any public or private school in this or any other state, the student must complete the entire term of the suspension or expulsion before being admitted into the school district. This policy may allow placement of the student in an alternative school program established under Article 13A of this Code, if available, for the remainder of the suspension or expulsion. Each public school and each private or nonpublic elementary or secondary school in this State shall within 10 days after the student has paid all of his or her outstanding fines and fees and at its own expense forward an official transcript of the scholastic records of each student transferring from that school in strict accordance with the provisions of this Section and the rules established by the State Board of Education as herein provided.

(b) The State Board of Education shall develop a one-page standard form that Illinois school districts are required to provide to any student who is moving out of the school district and that contains the information about whether or not the student is "in good standing" and whether or not his or her medical records are up-to-date and complete. As used in this Section, "in good standing" means that the student is not being disciplined by a suspension or expulsion, but is entitled to attend classes. No school district is required to admit a new student who is transferring from another Illinois school district unless he or she can produce the standard form from the student's previous school district enrollment. No school district is required to admit a new student who is transferring from an out-of-state public school unless the parent or guardian of the student certifies in writing that the student is not currently serving a suspension or expulsion imposed by the school from which the student is transferring.

(c) The State Board of Education shall, by rule, establish a system to provide for the accurate tracking of transfer students. This system shall, at a minimum, require that a student be counted as a dropout in the calculation of a school's or school district's annual student dropout rate unless the school or school district to which the student transferred (known hereafter in this subsection (c) as the transferee school or school district) sends notification to the school or school district from which the student transferred (known hereafter in this subsection (c) as the transferor school or school district) documenting that the student has enrolled in the transferee school or school district. This notification must occur within 150 days after the date the student withdraws from the transferor school or school district or the student shall be counted in the calculation of the transferor school's or school district's annual student dropout rate. A request by the transferee school or school district to the transferor school or school district seeking the student's academic transcripts or medical records shall be considered without limitation adequate documentation of enrollment. Each transferor school or school district shall keep documentation of such transfer students for the minimum period provided in the Illinois School Student Records Act. All records indicating the school or school district to which a student transferred are subject to the Illinois School Student Records Act.

Chapter 4

Safeguarding and Maintaining Student Records

"Ignorance of the law excuses no man."
– John Selde

In This Chapter:

4.1	Introduction
4.2	A Parent's Right to Access and Control the Student Record
4.3	The School's Obligation to Safeguard and Secure Student Records
4.4	The Records Custodian
4.5	Fees to Copy Records
4.6	Transfer of Student Records to Another School District
4.7	Transfer Student Records to Third Parties
4.8	Students Who Are 18
4.9	Dealing with Divorced Parents
4.10	Former Students
4.11	Electronic Grade Books
4.12	Student Biometric Information
4.13	Requests from the Military and Institutions of Higher Learning
4.14	Permanent and Temporary Records
4.15	Destruction of Records

FAQs
Sample Forms
References

4.1 Introduction

Student records are primarily governed by two different laws:

1. The Illinois School Student Records Act (ISSRA); and
2. The Federal Family Educational Rights and Privacy Act (FERPA).

ISSRA applies to all public elementary and secondary schools in Illinois, while FERPA applies to all public elementary and secondary schools and all private schools that receive federal funding. Hence, all Illinois public schools must follow both laws. Fortunately, ISSRA and FERPA are fairly similar. Therefore, in terms of the information below, this chapter will refer to ISSRA and FERPA jointly as the "student record acts."

Essentially, the student record acts govern safeguarding, control and access to education records. Education records (also called "student records") are defined as any document or other information that: (1) concerns and identifies a student; and (2) is maintained by a school or at the direction of a school employee. Specifically exempted from the definition of education records are teacher or administrator notes that are not shared with anyone except a substitute teacher and records maintained by law enforcement professionals working in a school.

This broad definition of education record includes not only records kept in a student's official file, but also includes such things as student pictures that are maintained by the school, emails that include student names and are sent through the district's computer server and student grades that are maintained on a district's computer system.

In a nutshell, the student record acts have two primary requirements: (1) a student's parent or guardian has the primary right to access and control their child's education record; and (2) schools must safeguard and secure all student records. These two rights and the exceptions are discussed more fully below.

4.2 A Parent's Right to Access and Control the Student Record

The student record acts grant to parents and eligible students (students 18 years of age and older) four primary rights. Notification of these rights must be made to parents and eligible students on a yearly basis. The actual means of notification (letter, student handbook, etc.) is left to the discretion of each school or district. Furthermore, school districts are required to notify in their native language parents who have a primary or home language other than English.

Parent / Student Right	Explanation
The right to inspect and review the student's education records maintained by the school.	A parent or eligible student must be granted access to the student record within a reasonable time, but in no case more than 15 days after making a request. Schools may charge a fee for copies, as discussed below.
The right to request that a school correct records which are believed to be inaccurate or misleading.	A parent or eligible student may ask the school to correct any records believed to be inaccurate or misleading. If the school determines that the record should not be amended, the parent or eligible student then has the right to a formal hearing. At the hearing the parent or eligible student must be given a full and fair opportunity to present evidence relevant to the issues raised and may, at their own expense, be assisted or represented by one or more individuals, including an attorney. After the hearing, if the school still decides not to amend the record, the parent or eligible student has the right to place a statement with the record setting forth his or her view of the contested information.

Parent / Student Right	**Explanation**
The right to prevent disclosure of the student's education record, subject to several exceptions.	This right provides that a parent or the eligible student must consent in writing whenever student record information is accessed or released or otherwise disclosed. This requirement is subject to several exceptions, which are discussed in detail in the next section.
The rights to complain to FERPA officials if any of the above rights are violated.	If a parent or eligible student believes that a school has violated the rights guaranteed by FERPA, a written complaint may be filed with the Family Compliance Office, U.S. Department of Education, 400 Maryland Ave. SW, Washington, DC 20202-4605. The Family Compliance Office investigates each complaint to determine whether the school district has failed to comply with the provisions of FERPA. Complaints must be filed with the Family Compliance Office within 180 days of the date of the alleged violation or the date that the complainant knew or reasonably should have known of the alleged violation.

4.3 The School's Obligation to Safeguard and Secure Student Records

Of the four rights discussed above, the right to prevent disclosure of a student's education record is perhaps the most widely used and debated. The student record acts generally provide that a student's education record and other documents governed by the acts cannot be released without written consent of the parent or eligible student. However, the acts allow schools to disclose student records, without consent, to certain parties or under certain circumstances. These exceptions include:

- To school officials with a current demonstrable educational interest in the student. This generally includes school and district administrators, a student's current teachers, other educational professionals working with the student and coaches of athletic teams on which the student is participating. Schools and school districts must use "reasonable methods" to assure that education records are not released to school officials who do not have a legitimate educational interest in a student.

- To other schools where a student is transferring or has transferred. Here, the student's parent or the eligible student must be notified in advance of the record information being sent, receive a copy of the student record if desired and have an opportunity for a hearing to challenge the content of the record.

- To individuals for certain research and statistical reporting, provided that personal student identifiers are removed.

- To comply with a court order, provided the parent or eligible student is given prompt notice. Note that a court order is a directive from a court and contains a judge's signature. A subpoena signed by a court clerk, attorney or administrative agency official is not a court order unless also signed by a judge.
- To juvenile justice authorities, when necessary to discharge their official duties.
- To appropriate persons in the case of an articulable and significant threat to the health or safety of a student, provided the student's parent is notified the next school day.
- To a governmental or social service agency investigating a student's attendance.
- To specified officials for audit or evaluation purposes.
- Pursuant to an established policy on directory information. Here, schools may disclose, without consent, directory information, which may include a student's name, picture, address, telephone listing, date and place of birth, major field of study, participation in officially recognized activities and sports, weight and height of members of athletic teams, dates of attendance, degrees and awards received and the most recent school attended by the student. However, schools must tell parents and eligible students what the school considers to be directory information, and allow parents and eligible students a reasonable amount of time to request that the school not disclose directory information about the student.

4.4 The Records Custodian

Each school must appoint a records custodian to assure that requirements of the student record acts are followed. In most school districts, the records custodian is the school principal. In reality, however, the school secretary generally has primary responsibility over student records and recordkeeping. The record custodian's general responsibilities include: (1) safeguarding student records; (2) maintaining accurate records whenever a student's record is accessed or released to a third party; and (3) assuring that information is properly added and removed from each student record. In order to help maintain accurate records, we recommend – and to some extent schools are required to keep – two separate record logs. The first record log, which we call the "Student Record Access Log," records the name of any person who accesses a student's records along with other information. It is recommended that this log be kept near the permanent and temporary record files. The second log, which we call the "Record Release Form," is used to note any time that a student's education record (or part of the record) is copied and distributed to third parties. A sample Student Record Access Log (Form 4-4) and Record Release Form (Form 4-5) are found at the end of this chapter.

4.5 Fees to Copy Records

The school may charge the actual cost of providing a copy of the student record or any portion of the record, provided that the cost does not exceed $.35 per page. No parent or student may be denied a copy of a student's records due to inability to pay the cost of copying.

4.6 Transfer of Student Records to Another School District

If a school receives notification that a student is seeking enrollment in another school district, the school that the student is leaving is obligated to send certain student record documents to the new school. Specifically, an unofficial copy of the student's transcript must be sent to the new school within 10 days of that school's request. The remainder of the student's record must then be sent to the new school. Only a student's official academic transcript may be withheld if the student owes money to the school district. All other student record information MUST be sent to the new school district. (Note, only copies of records should be forwarded. Original records should be retained by the district.)

In addition, the sending school must forward to the new school a completed student in good standing form. This form, as discussed below, indicates whether or not the student is currently excluded from school due to a suspension or expulsion, and whether the student's medical records are up-to-date. This form can, for the sake of time and convenience, be faxed to the new school.

4.7 Transfer of Student Records to Third Parties

In cases where personally identifiable information from an education record is properly released to a third party, that party must agree not to further release the information without the written consent of the parent or eligible student. If a third party permits access to information in violation of the student record acts or fails to destroy information as required, the school district is prohibited from permitting access to information from education records to that third party for a period of not less than five years.

4.8 Students Who Are 18

As first discussed above, when a student turns 18 years of age, he or she becomes an "eligible student" and all rights otherwise accorded to the parents are transferred to the student. If an eligible student requests, school officials must communicate directly with the eligible student regarding his or her education records.

Note that ISSRA also provides that a school must allow all students the ability to view and copy their permanent record file. A school district may also permit a student under 18 to view the student's temporary record file. However, when the student is under 18, the student's parent must make all educational decisions on behalf of the student.

4.9 Dealing with Divorced Parents

Frequently, divorced parents try to put the school in the middle when it comes to disagreements over raising their child. For example, one parent may argue that the other parent does not have the right to attend parent-teacher conferences or receive a copy of the student's report card. The general rule of thumb is that both parents (regardless of their circumstances) have the right to access their child's record and otherwise participate in their child's education. This includes the right to receive report cards, inquire whether or not the student is in attendance on a particular day, attend parent-teacher conferences and review the student's Individualized Education Program, if applicable.

Although both parents have the right to participate in their child's education, only the custodial parent has the right to make educational decisions on behalf of the child. Determining which parent is the custodial parent can often be difficult, especially when both parents are claiming that they are "in charge" of their child. In these situations, it is important for the school to request copies of the divorce decree (if applicable) and any court orders relative to parenting and custody. These documents are often helpful in determining the rights of the parties. Note, that if there is ever a discrepancy over which parent is the custodial parent, you can deny both parents access to their child's education record for up to 15 days, which should give the school ample time to sort out the situation.

4.10 Former Students

The student record acts should be viewed as protecting the rights of students who have graduated or left the school district for any other reason. The student record acts do not, however, protect the rights of deceased students. A school or district has complete discretion as to whether or not to release information concerning a deceased former student. If a school or district consents to release information on a deceased former student, a death certificate or other proof of death should be required.

4.11 Electronic Grade Books

Another major concern of the electronic age is the use of computer-based grade books and attendance systems. Again, it is important to remember that these tools create student records to the extent that they identify students and are maintained by the school. Schools should assure that this information is strictly safeguarded and password protected. Only individuals with a legitimate educational interest or other legal need to know should have access to this information, no matter where such information is stored.

4.12 Student Biometric Information

Before collecting biometric information from students, the school must seek the permission of the student's parent or the student, if over the age of 18. Biometric information means information that is collected from students based on their unique characteristics, such as a fingerprint, voice recognition or retinal scan.

4.13 Requests from the Military and Institutions of Higher Learning

Upon their request, military recruiters and institutions of higher learning must be given access to students' names, addresses and telephone numbers. Parents who do not want their child's name and information to be released (or students over the age of 18 who do not want their name and information released) can notify the school that they do not want any information released to the military or institutions of higher education.

4.14 Permanent and Temporary Records

Illinois law also requires student records to be divided into two categories: permanent records and temporary records. Permanent records must be kept for a minimum of 60 years and temporary records must be kept for a minimum of five years after the student graduates or otherwise leaves the school district. The information contained in permanent and temporary records is as follows:

Permanent Record	Temporary Record
<u>Must</u> include: • Basic identifying information, including the student's name and address, birth date and place, gender, and the names and addresses of the student's parents	<u>Must</u> include: • Information regarding discipline, a suspension or an expulsions for drugs, weapons or bodily harm to another • Scores on state assessment tests in grades K through 8 only • A record release form

Permanent Record	Temporary Record
• Academic transcripts, including grades, class rank, graduation date, grade level achieved, and scores on college entrance examinations • Attendance records • Health records (defined as those medical documents necessary for enrollment) • Scores on state assessment tests in grades 9 through 12 only	• Reports of "indicated" physical or sexual abuse from DCFS • Health-related records (defined as medical records, other than those necessary for enrollment) • Accident reports • The completed home language survey form • Any biometric information that is collected by the school
<u>May</u> Include: • Honors and awards • Information concerning participation in school-sponsored activities or athletics, or offices held in school-sponsored organizations <u>No other information may be placed in the permanent record.</u>	<u>May</u> include: • Family background information • Intelligence scores • Aptitude tests • Reports of psychological evaluations • Honors and awards • Participation in school events • Teacher notes • Other disciplinary information • Special education files • 504 plans and documents Any other verified information that is clearly relevant to the student's education may be placed in the temporary record.

4.15 Destruction of Records

Before any school district record is destroyed, the school district must comply with the Illinois Local Records Act. This Act requires that a school district obtain official permission from the Illinois Secretary of State's office before removing and destroying records. Essentially, the Local Records Act requires that a school district comply with the following steps:

- The Secretary of State's local records unit must be contacted
- The above office must approve all records to be destroyed
- A records disposal certificate must be prepared by the Secretary of State's office
- The above certificate must be submitted to the local records commission for approval 60 days in advance of record destruction
- Upon approval by the local records commission, the records may be destroyed, but only after the school district provides reasonable prior notice to parents and eligible students of the information that the school district intends to destroy

FAQs

What is an education record or student record?

Education records (also called "student records") are defined as any document or other information that (1) concerns and identifies a student; and (2) is maintained by a school or at the direction of a school employee. Specifically exempted from the definition of education records are teacher or administrator notes that are not shared with anyone except a substitute teacher and records maintained by law enforcement professionals working in a school.

Who has access to a student's record?

Generally, a student's parent and school staff with a current demonstrable educational interest in the student have access to a student's record. There are numerous exceptions to this general rule. For more information, see Sections 4.3.

What is a permanent student record?

A student's permanent record contains personal information necessary for the school to educate the student. For a list of information required to be in a student's permanent record, see Section 4.14.

What is a temporary student record?

A student's temporary record contains information important to a student's education. For a list of information that should be placed in a student's temporary record, see Section 4.14.

What is directory information?

Directory information is general information about a student, and may include a student's name, photo, address, telephone listing, date and place of birth, photographs and videos used for informational or news-related purposes, major field of study, participation in officially recognized activities and sports, weight and height of members of athletic teams, dates of attendance, degrees and awards received and the most recent school attended by the student. Schools may disclose directory information without parent consent. However, schools must tell parents and eligible students what constitutes directory information and allow parents and eligible students a reasonable amount of time to request that the school not disclose any directory information about the student.

What is student biometric information?

Biometric information means information that is collected from students based on their unique characteristics, such as a fingerprint, voice recognition or retinal scan. Before collecting biometric information from students, the school must seek the permission of the student's parent or the student, if over the age of 18.

How long does a school have to maintain a student's record?

Permanent records must be maintained by a school district for a period of at least 60 years after a student has graduated or otherwise left the school district. Temporary records must be maintained for at least five years after a student has graduated or otherwise left the school district.

What are the procedures for transferring a student's record to another school district?
When a student transfers to a new school district, the sending school must immediately forward an unofficial copy of the student's transcript and the student in good standing form. The remainder of the student's record must then be sent to the new school. For more information, see Section 4.6.

What are the consequences for violating the student record acts?
Willful failure to comply with ISSRA is a petty offense, while willful or malicious falsification of student record information is a Class A misdemeanor.

Do the student record acts apply to former students?
The student record acts should be viewed as protecting the rights of students who have graduated or left the school district for any other reason. The student record acts do not, however, protect the rights of deceased students. For more information, see Section 4.10.

Are schools required to give student information to military recruiters?
Upon their request, military recruiters must be given access to students' names, addresses and telephone numbers. Parents who do not want their child's name and information to be released (or students over the age of 18 who do not want their name and information released) can notify the school that they do not any information released to the military.

Should I send a student's record to his or her new school if the student owes our school money?
In cases where a student owes the school money, the school may only withhold the student's official academic transcript. All other documents, including the student's unofficial student transcript, must be forwarded to a student's new school or college.

Do State assessment tests (like ISAT and PSAE) go in the permanent or temporary record?
Standardized tests for grades K-8 are maintained in a student's temporary file, while standardized tests for grades 9-12 are maintained in a student's permanent file.

If I am entering information in all student files or updating all student files, do I have to complete the Student Record Access Log?
When entering mass data, only one entry needs to be made in the Student Record Access Log. For example, under "student" the school secretary could simply write "all."

Who has the rights to a student's records when the student turns 18 years old?
When a student turns 18 years of age, he or she becomes an "eligible student" and all rights otherwise accorded to the parents are transferred to the student. For more information, see Section 4.8.

Can I destroy student records that are out of date?

Student records (and all other school district records) must be destroyed in accordance with State law and the Local Records Act. This requires a school district to seek and obtain permission from the Illinois Secretary of State's office before any records are destroyed. School staff should consult with their principal on specific district procedures for destruction of records. For more information, see Section 4.15.

When I send a student record to a new school district, do I send the originals or a copy?

If a student is moving from one school to another in the same district, the original student record should be sent to the new school. However, if the student is transferring to another school district a copy of the student's record should be sent to the new district.

In the case of divorced parents, who has the right to student records?

Both the custodial parent and the non-custodial parent have the right to access and view their child's education record. However, only the custodial parent has the right to make educational decisions. If there are any questions as to who the custodial parent is and who the non-custodial parent is, the school secretary should defer to the principal, who should then request appropriate documentation from the parties.

Can a parent designate a third-party to review a student's education record?

Yes. A parent can designate to a third-party the right to access his or her child's education record. All designations should be made in writing.

Can a school charge a fee to copy a student's record?

The school may charge the actual cost of providing a copy of the student record or any portion of the record, provided that the cost does not exceed $.35 per page. No parent or student may be denied a copy of a student's records due to inability to pay the cost of copying.

What is a student in good standing form?

This is a State mandated form that must be sent when a student transfers to a new school district. The form indicates whether or not the student's medical records are up-to-date and whether or not the student is currently serving a suspension or expulsion from the student's former school district. For more information, see sample Form 4-3.

Sample Forms

Sample forms available at www.edlawyer.org

Sample Form 4-1: Model Student Handbook Student Record Notification
(This information should be placed in the school's student handbook or otherwise provided to parents and eligible students on a yearly basis.

Student Records
School student records are confidential and information from them will not be released other than as provided by law.

The school and district routinely discloses "directory" type information without consent. Directory information is limited to: name, address, gender, grade level, birth date and place, parents' names and address; academic awards, degrees and honors; information in relation to school-sponsored activities, organizations, and athletics; major field of study; and period of attendance at the school. Any parent/guardian or eligible student (student 18 or older) may prohibit the release of directory information by delivering a written request to the building principal.

State and Federal law gives parents and eligible students certain rights with respect to their student records. These rights are:

1. The right to inspect and copy the student's education records within 15 school days of the day the school receives a request for access. There may be a small charge for copies, not to exceed $.35 per page. This fee will be waived for those unable to afford such cost.

2. The right to request the amendment of the portion student's education record that the parent/guardian or eligible student believes is inaccurate, misleading, irrelevant, or improper.

3. The right to permit disclosure of personally identifiable information contained in the student's education records, except in certain circumstances. Disclosure is permitted without consent in the case of directory information and to school officials with legitimate educational or administrative interests. Disclosure is also permitted without consent to: any person for research, statistical reporting or planning, provided that no student or parent/guardian can be identified; any person named in a court order; appropriate persons if the knowledge of such information is necessary to protect the health or safety of the student or other persons; juvenile authorities when necessary for the discharge of their official duties who request information before adjudication of the student; and in other cases permitted by law.

4. The right to complain to the U.S. Department of Education if the school or district fails to comply with the above. Federal officials can be contacted at:
Family Policy Compliance Office
U.S. Department of Education
400 Maryland Avenue. SW
Washington, D.C. 20202-4605

Used with Permission from Illinois Principals Association, Model Student Handbook, Procedure 11.20 (09/09)

Sample Form 4-2: Using a Photograph or Video Recording of a Student

(This Distribute to parent(s)/guardian(s) at the time they register a child for school and/or annually at the beginning of the school year. Return to the Building Principal to be kept in the student's temporary record.)

Student _____ School year _____

• Pictures of Unnamed Students

Students may occasionally appear in photographs and video recordings taken by school staff members, other students, or other individuals authorized by the Building Principal. The school may use these pictures, without identifying the student, in various publications, including the school yearbook, school newspaper, and school website. No consent or notice is needed or will be given before the school uses pictures of unnamed students taken while they are at school or a school-related activity.

• Pictures of Named Students

Sometimes the school may want to identify a student in a school picture. For example, school officials want to acknowledge those students who participate in a school activity or deserve special recognition.

In order for the school to publish a picture with a student identified by name, one of the student's parents or guardians must sign the consent below. Please complete and sign this form to allow the school to publish and otherwise use photographs and video recordings, with your child identified, while he or she is enrolled in this school.

I grant consent to the School District to identify a picture of my child, by full name and/or the school he or she attends, in any school sponsored material, publication, video recording, or website. This consent is valid for the entire time my child is enrolled in the District. I may revoke this consent at any time by notifying the Building Principal.

_____
Parent/Guardian signature

_____
Parent/Guardian signature

_____
Date

• Pictures of Students Taken By Non-School Agencies

While the school limits access to school buildings by outside photographers, it has no control over news media or other entities that may publish a picture of a named or unnamed student. School staff members will not, however, identify a student for an outside photographer.

Used with Permission from Illinois Association of School Boards, PRESS Form7:340, E2
(05/06)

Sample Form 4-3: Student Transfer Form

ILLINOIS STATE BOARD OF EDUCATION
Educator and School Development Division
100 North First Street, E-310
Springfield, Illinois 62777-0001

STUDENT IDENTIFICATION NUMBER (9-digits)

STUDENT TRANSFER FORM

In accordance with Section 2-3.13a of the School Code, all public school districts are to provide this form to any student who is moving out of the school district to verify whether or not the student is "in good standing" and, whether or not their medical records are up-to-date and complete as defined in Section 2-3.13a. "In good standing" means that the student is not being disciplined by an out-of-school suspension or expulsion, and is entitled to attend classes, as of the date of this form. No public school district is required to admit a new student unless they can produce this form from the student's previous Illinois public school district. **This form is not to be returned to the Illinois State Board of Education. It is to be sent directly to the student's new school they will be attending.**

NAME OF STUDENT (Last, First, Middle)	BIRTHDATE (Month, Day, Year)	GENDER ☐ Male ☐ Female	GRADE LEVEL

ADDRESS OF STUDENT (Street, City, State, Zip Code)

NAME OF PARENT OR GUARDIAN	PARENT/GUARDIAN TELEPHONE (Include Area Code)
	Home Work

ADDRESS OF PARENT OR GUARDIAN (Street, City, State, Zip Code)

DISTRICT NAME AND NUMBER TRANSFERRING TO	NEW DISTRICT ADDRESS (City, State, Zip Code)

NAME OF SCHOOL STUDENT WILL BE TRANSFERRING TO	NAME OF PRINCIPAL AT NEW SCHOOL

Please check (✓) the appropriate box.

☐ I hereby attest that the above student is "in good standing" and that all medical records for the above student are up-to-date and complete as of the date of this form.

☐ The above student's medical records are **not** up-to-date and complete as documented in the student's permanent records.

☐ I hereby attest that the above student is **not** "in good standing" due to a current suspension and/or expulsion from _____ until _____; but is entitled to transfer in accordance with Section 2-3.13a (105 ILCS 5/2-3.13a), unless the receiving district has, pursuant to Section 2-3.13a, adopted a policy providing that if a student is suspended or expelled for any reason from any public or private school in this or any other state, the student must complete the entire term of the suspension or expulsion before being admitted into the school district. This policy may allow placement of the student in an alternative school program established under Article 13A of this Code, if available, for the remainder of the suspension or expulsion.

☐ I hereby attest that the above student is **not** "in good standing" due to a current suspension and/or expulsion from _____ until _____ and is **not** eligible for transfer for knowingly possessing in a school building or on school grounds a weapon as defined in the Gun Free Schools Act (20 U.S.C. 8921 et seq.); for knowingly possessing, selling, or delivering in a school building or on school grounds a controlled substance or cannabis; or for battering a staff member of the school.

NAME OF PRINCIPAL	SCHOOL PHONE	COUNTY

DISTRICT NAME AND NUMBER	DISTRICT ADDRESS (City, State, Zip Code)

_____ _____
Date   Signature of Principal

ISBE 33-78 (8/11)   **THIS FORM IS TO BE SENT DIRECTLY TO THE STUDENT'S NEW SCHOOL THEY WILL BE ATTENDING.**

Illinois State Board of Education Form 33-78 (8/11)

Sample Form 4-4: Student Record Access log

(This form should be kept with the temporary and permanent records and completed any time that these records are accessed.)

All individuals accessing a student record MUST complete the following information. For mass entries (such as updating records or inserting standard testing documents) a single entry may be made indicating the purpose of the access.

Date of Record Entry	Name of Student	Individual Seeking Access	Purpose for Accessing Student Record	Signature of Individual Seeking Access

Sample Form 4-5: Sample Record Release Form

(This document should be kept in the temporary file and completed any time that student record information is released.)

Student Name: _____ Student ID Number: _____
Parent / Guardian Name: _____

Information Released to (full name and address)	Description of Info (including format)	Reason for Release	Date of Record Release	Name & Signature of Records Custodian	Name & Signature of Records Custodian	Parent Notification (attach release)

References

105 ILCS 5/2-3.13a. School Records; Transferring Students.

(a) The State Board of Education shall establish and implement rules requiring all of the public schools and all private or nonpublic elementary and secondary schools located in this State, whenever any such school has a student who is transferring to any other public elementary or secondary school located in this or in any other state, to forward within 10 days of notice of the student's transfer an unofficial record of that student's grades to the school to which such student is transferring. Each public school at the same time also shall forward to the school to which the student is transferring the remainder of the student's school student records as required by the Illinois School Student Records Act. In addition, if a student is transferring from a public school, whether located in this or any other state, from which the student has been suspended or expelled for knowingly possessing in a school building or on school grounds a weapon as defined in the Gun Free Schools Act, for knowingly possessing, selling, or delivering in a school building or on school grounds a controlled substance or cannabis, or for battering a staff member of the school, and if the period of suspension or expulsion has not expired at the time the student attempts to transfer into another public school in the same or any other school district: (i) any school student records required to be transferred shall include the date and duration of the period of suspension or expulsion; and (ii) with the exception of transfers into the Department of Juvenile Justice school district, the student shall not be permitted to attend class in the public school into which he or she is transferring until the student has served the entire period of the suspension or expulsion imposed by the school from which the student is transferring, provided that the school board may approve the placement of the student in an alternative school program established under Article 13A of this Code. A school district may adopt a policy providing that if a student is suspended or expelled for any reason from any public or private school in this or any other state, the student must complete the entire term of the suspension or expulsion before being admitted into the school district. This policy may allow placement of the student in an alternative school program established under Article 13A of this Code, if available, for the remainder of the suspension or expulsion. Each public school and each private or nonpublic elementary or secondary school in this State shall within 10 days after the student has paid all of his or her outstanding fines and fees and at its own expense forward an official transcript of the scholastic records of each student transferring from that school in strict accordance with the provisions of this Section and the rules established by the State Board of Education as herein provided.

(b) The State Board of Education shall develop a one-page standard form that Illinois school districts are required to provide to any student who is moving out of the school district and that contains the information about whether or not the student is "in good standing" and whether or not his or her medical records are up-to-date and complete. As used in this Section, "in good standing" means that the student is not being disciplined by a suspension or expulsion, but is entitled to attend classes. No school district is required to admit a new student who is transferring from another Illinois school district unless he or she can produce the standard form from the student's previous school district enrollment. No school district is required to admit a new student who is transferring from an out-of-state public school unless the parent or guardian of the student certifies in writing that the student is not currently serving a suspension or expulsion imposed by the school from which the student is transferring.

(c) The State Board of Education shall, by rule, establish a system to provide for the accurate tracking of transfer students. This system shall, at a minimum, require that a student be counted as a dropout in the calculation of a school's or school district's annual student dropout rate unless the school or school district to which the student transferred (known hereafter in this subsection (c) as the transferee school or school district) sends notification to the school or school district from which the student transferred (known hereafter in this subsection (c) as the transferor school or school district) documenting that the student has enrolled in the transferee school or school district. This notification must occur within 150 days after the date the student withdraws from the transferor school or school district or the student shall be counted in the calculation of the transferor school's or school district's annual student dropout rate. A request by the transferee school or school district to the transferor school or school district seeking the student's academic transcripts or medical records shall be considered without limitation adequate documentation of enrollment. Each transferor school or school district shall keep documentation of such transfer students for the minimum period provided in the Illinois School Student Records Act. All records indicating the school or school district to which a student transferred are subject to the Illinois School Student Records Act.

105 ILCS 10/1, *et. seq.* Illinois School Student Records Act.

10/1 Short title
This Act shall be known and may be cited as the Illinois School Student Records Act.

10/2. Definitions
As used in this Act,

(a) "Student" means any person enrolled or previously enrolled in a school.

(b) "School" means any public preschool, day care center, kindergarten, nursery, elementary or secondary educational institution, vocational school, special educational facility or any other elementary or secondary educational agency or institution and any person, agency or institution which maintains school student records from more than one school, but does not include a private or non-public school.

(c) "State Board" means the State Board of Education.

(d) "School Student Record" means any writing or other recorded information concerning a student and by which a student may be individually identified, maintained by a school or at its direction or by an employee of a school, regardless of how or where the information is stored. The following shall not be deemed school student records under this Act: writings or other recorded information maintained by an employee of a school or other person at the direction of a school for his or her exclusive use; provided that all such writings and other recorded information are destroyed not later than the student's graduation or permanent withdrawal from the school; and provided further that no such records or recorded information may be released or disclosed to any person except a person designated by the school as a substitute unless they are first incorporated in a school student record and made subject to all of the provisions of this Act. School student records shall not include information maintained by law enforcement professionals working in the school.

(e) "Student Permanent Record" means the minimum personal information necessary to a school in the education of the student and contained in a school student record. Such information may include the student's name, birth date, address, grades and grade level, parents' names and addresses, attendance records, and such other entries as the State Board may require or authorize.

(f) "Student Temporary Record" means all information contained in a school student record but not contained in the student permanent record. Such information may include family background information, intelligence test scores, aptitude test scores, psychological and personality test results, teacher evaluations, and other information of clear relevance to the education of the student, all subject to regulations of the State Board. The information shall include information provided under Section 8.6 of the Abused and Neglected Child Reporting Act. In addition, the student temporary record shall include information regarding serious disciplinary infractions that resulted in expulsion, suspension, or the imposition of punishment or sanction. For purposes of this provision, serious disciplinary infractions means: infractions involving drugs, weapons, or bodily harm to another.

(g) "Parent" means a person who is the natural parent of the student or other person who has the primary responsibility for the care and upbringing of the student. All rights and privileges accorded to a parent under this Act shall become exclusively those of the student upon his 18th birthday, graduation from secondary school, marriage or entry into military service, whichever occurs first. Such rights and privileges may also be exercised by the student at any time with respect to the student's permanent school record.

10/3. Rules and regulations

(a) The State Board shall issue regulations to govern the contents of school student records, to implement and assure compliance with the provisions of this Act and to prescribe appropriate procedures and forms for all administrative proceedings, notices and consents required or permitted under this Act. All such regulations and any rules and regulations adopted by any school relating to the maintenance of, access to, dissemination of or challenge to school student records shall be available to the general public.

(b) The State Board, each local school board or other governing body and each school shall take reasonable measures to assure that all persons accorded rights or obligations under this Act are informed of such rights and obligations.

(c) The principal of each school or the person with like responsibilities or his or her designate shall take all action necessary to assure that school personnel are informed of the provisions of this Act.

10/4. Custodian; permanent and temporary records

(a) Each school shall designate an official records custodian who is responsible for the maintenance, care and security of all school student records, whether or not such records are in his personal custody or control.

(b) The official records custodian shall take all reasonable measures to prevent unauthorized access to or dissemination of school student records.

(c) Information contained in or added to a school student record shall be limited to information which is of clear relevance to the education of the student.

(d) Information added to a student temporary record after the effective date of this Act shall include the name, signature and position of the person who has added such information and the date of its entry into the record.

(e) Each school shall maintain student permanent records and the information contained therein for not less than 60 years after the student has transferred, graduated or otherwise permanently withdrawn from the school.

(f) Each school shall maintain student temporary records and the information contained in those records for not less than 5 years after the student has transferred, graduated, or otherwise withdrawn from the school. However, student temporary records shall not be disclosed except as provided in Section 5 or 6 or by court order. A school may maintain indefinitely anonymous information from student temporary records for authorized research, statistical reporting or planning purposes, provided that no student or parent can be individually identified from the information maintained.

(g) The principal of each school or the person with like responsibilities or his or her designate shall periodically review each student temporary record for verification of entries and elimination or correction of all inaccurate, misleading, unnecessary or irrelevant information. The State Board shall issue regulations to govern the periodic review of the student temporary records and length of time for maintenance of entries to such records.

(h) Before any school student record is destroyed or information deleted therefrom, the parent shall be given reasonable prior notice at his or her last known address in accordance with regulations adopted by the State Board and an opportunity to copy the record and information proposed to be destroyed or deleted.

(i) No school shall be required to separate permanent and temporary school student records of a student not enrolled in such school on or after the effective date of this Act or to destroy any such records, or comply with the provisions of paragraph (g) of this Section with respect to such records, except (1) in accordance with the request of the parent that any or all of such actions be taken in compliance with the provisions of this Act or (2) in accordance with regulations adopted by the State Board.

10/5. Inspection and access

(a) A parent or any person specifically designated as a representative by a parent shall have the right to inspect and copy all school student permanent and temporary records of that parent's child. A student shall have the right to inspect and copy his or her school student permanent record. No person who is prohibited by an order of protection from inspecting or obtaining school records of a student pursuant to the Illinois Domestic Violence Act of 1986, as now or hereafter amended, shall have any right of access to, or inspection of, the school records of that student. If a school's principal or person with like responsibilities or his designee has knowledge of such order of protection, the school shall prohibit access or inspection of the student's school records by such person.

(b) Whenever access to any person is granted pursuant to paragraph (a) of this Section, at the option of either the parent or the school a qualified professional, who may be a psychologist, counselor or other advisor, and who may be an employee of the school or employed by the parent, may be present to interpret the information contained in the student temporary record. If the school requires that a professional be present, the school shall secure and bear any cost of the presence of the professional. If the parent so requests, the school shall secure and bear any cost of the presence of a professional employed by the school.

(c) A parent's or student's request to inspect and copy records, or to allow a specifically designated representative to inspect and copy records, must be granted within a reasonable time, and in no case later than 15 school days after the date of receipt of such request by the official records custodian.

(d) The school may charge its reasonable costs for the copying of school student records, not to exceed the amounts fixed in schedules adopted by the State Board, to any person permitted to copy such records, except that no parent or student shall be denied a copy of school student records as permitted under this Section 5 for inability to bear the cost of such copying.

(e) Nothing contained in this Section 5 shall make available to a parent or student confidential letters and statements of recommendation furnished in connection with applications for employment to a post-secondary educational institution or the receipt of an honor or honorary recognition, provided such letters and statements are not used for purposes other than those for which they were specifically intended, and

   (1) were placed in a school student record prior to January 1, 1975; or

   (2) the student has waived access thereto after being advised of his right to obtain upon request the names of all such persons making such confidential recommendations.

(f) Nothing contained in this Act shall be construed to impair or limit the confidentiality of:

   (1) Communications otherwise protected by law as privileged or confidential, including but not limited to, information communicated in confidence to a physician, psychologist or other psychotherapist, school social worker, school counselor, school psychologist, or school social worker, school counselor, or school psychologist intern who works under the direct supervision of a school social worker, school counselor, or school psychologist; or

   (2) Information which is communicated by a student or parent in confidence to school personnel; or

(3) Information which is communicated by a student, parent, or guardian to a law enforcement professional working in the school, except as provided by court order.

(g) No school employee shall be subjected to adverse employment action, the threat of adverse employment action, or any manner of discrimination because the employee is acting or has acted to protect communications as privileged or confidential pursuant to applicable provisions of State or federal law or rule or regulation.

10/6. Parties entitled to access; notice to parents; record of release; consent

(a) No school student records or information contained therein may be released, transferred, disclosed or otherwise disseminated, except as follows:

(1) To a parent or student or person specifically designated as a representative by a parent, as provided in paragraph (a) of Section 5;

(2) To an employee or official of the school or school district or State Board with current demonstrable educational or administrative interest in the student, in furtherance of such interest;

(3) To the official records custodian of another school within Illinois or an official with similar responsibilities of a school outside Illinois, in which the student has enrolled, or intends to enroll, upon the request of such official or student;

(4) To any person for the purpose of research, statistical reporting, or planning, provided that such research, statistical reporting, or planning is permissible under and undertaken in accordance with the federal Family Educational Rights and Privacy Act);

(5) Pursuant to a court order, provided that the parent shall be given prompt written notice upon receipt of such order of the terms of the order, the nature and substance of the information proposed to be released in compliance with such order and an opportunity to inspect and copy the school student records and to challenge their contents pursuant to Section 7;

(6) To any person as specifically required by State or federal law;

(6.5) To juvenile authorities when necessary for the discharge of their official duties who request information prior to adjudication of the student and who certify in writing that the information will not be disclosed to any other party except as provided under law or order of court. For purposes of this Section "juvenile authorities" means: (i) a judge of the circuit court and members of the staff of the court designated by the judge; (ii) parties to the proceedings under the Juvenile Court Act of 1987 and their attorneys; (iii) probation officers and court appointed advocates for the juvenile authorized by the judge hearing the case; (iv) any individual, public or private agency having custody of the child pursuant to court order; (v) any individual, public or private agency providing education, medical or mental health service to the child when the requested information is needed to determine the appropriate service or treatment for the minor; (vi) any potential placement provider when such release is authorized by the court for the limited purpose of determining the appropriateness of the potential placement; (vii) law enforcement officers and prosecutors; (viii) adult and juvenile prisoner review boards; (ix) authorized military personnel; (x) individuals authorized by court;

(7) Subject to regulations of the State Board, in connection with an emergency, to appropriate persons if the knowledge of such information is necessary to protect the health or safety of the student or other persons;

(8) To any person, with the prior specific dated written consent of the parent designating the person to whom the records may be released, provided that at the time any such consent is requested or obtained, the parent shall be advised in writing that he has the right to inspect and copy such records in accordance with Section 5, to challenge their contents in accordance with Section 7 and to limit any such consent to designated records or designated portions of the information contained therein;

(9) To a governmental agency, or social service agency contracted by a governmental agency, in furtherance of an investigation of a student's school attendance pursuant to the compulsory student attendance laws of this State, provided that the records are released to the employee or agent designated by the agency;

(10) To those SHOCAP committee members who fall within the meaning of "state and local officials and authorities," as those terms are used within the meaning of the federal Family Educational Rights and Privacy Act, for the purposes of identifying serious habitual juvenile offenders and matching those offenders with community resources pursuant to Section 5-145 of the Juvenile Court Act of 1987, but only to the extent that the release, transfer, disclosure, or dissemination is consistent with the Family Educational Rights and Privacy Act;

(11) To the Department of Healthcare and Family Services in furtherance of the requirements of Section 2-3.131, 3-14.29, 10-28, or 34-18.26 of the School Code or Section 10 of the School Breakfast and Lunch Program Act; or

(12) To the State Board or another State government agency or between or among State government agencies in order to evaluate or audit federal and State programs or perform research and planning, but only to the extent that the release, transfer, disclosure, or dissemination is consistent with the federal Family Educational Rights and Privacy Act

(b) No information may be released pursuant to subparagraphs (3) or (6) of paragraph (a) of this Section 6 unless the parent receives prior written notice of the nature and substance of the information proposed to be released, and an opportunity to inspect and copy such records in accordance with Section 5 and to challenge their contents in accordance with Section 7. Provided, however, that such notice shall be sufficient if published in a local newspaper of general circulation or other publication directed generally to the parents involved where the proposed release of information is pursuant to subparagraph 6 of paragraph (a) in this Section 6 and relates to more than 25 students.

(c) A record of any release of information pursuant to this Section must be made and kept as a part of the school student record and subject to the access granted by Section 5. Such record of release shall be maintained for the life of the school student records and shall be available only to the parent and the official records custodian. Each record of release shall also include:

(1) The nature and substance of the information released;

(2) The name and signature of the official records custodian releasing such information;

(3) The name of the person requesting such information, the capacity in which such a request has been made, and the purpose of such request;

(4) The date of the release; and

(5) A copy of any consent to such release.

(d) Except for the student and his parents, no person to whom information is released pursuant to this Section and no person specifically designated as a representative by a parent may permit any other person to have access to such information without a prior consent of the parent obtained in accordance with the requirements of subparagraph (8) of paragraph (a) of this Section.

(e) Nothing contained in this Act shall prohibit the publication of student directories which list student names, addresses and other identifying information and similar publications which comply with regulations issued by the State Board.

10/7. Challenges

(a) Parents shall have the right to challenge the accuracy, relevance or propriety of any entry in the school student records, exclusive of (i) academic grades of their child and (ii) references to expulsions or out-of-school suspensions, if the challenge is made at the time the student's school student records are forwarded to another school to which the student is transferring.

(b) The State Board shall prescribe by regulation procedures to govern challenges to school student records under this Act. Such challenge procedures shall provide for a hearing at which each party shall have:

(1) The right to present evidence and to call witnesses;

(2) The right to cross-examine witnesses;

(3) The right to counsel;

(4) The right to a written statement of any decision and the reasons therefore;

(5) The right to appeal an adverse decision to an administrative tribunal or official to be established or designated by the State Board.

(c) A final decision under the procedures established pursuant to this Section may be appealed to the Circuit Court of the County in which the school is located.

(d) Parents shall also have the right to insert in their child's school student record a statement of reasonable length setting forth their position on any disputed information contained in that record. The school shall include a copy of such statement in any subsequent dissemination of the information in dispute.

10/8. Rights conditioned on securing information from temporary records

No person may condition the granting or withholding of any right, privilege or benefit or make as a condition of employment, credit or insurance the securing by any individual of any information from a student's temporary record which such individual may obtain through the exercise of any right secured under this Act.

10/8.1. Presentation of school student record or Individualized Education Program to receiving school district

(a) No school may refuse to admit or enroll a student because of that student's failure to present his student permanent or temporary record from a school previously attended.

(b) When a new student applies for admission to a school and does not present his school student record, such school may notify the school or school district last attended by such student, requesting that the student's school student record be copied and sent to it; such request shall be honored within 10 days after it is received. Within 10 days after receiving a request from the Department of Children and Family Services, the school district last attended by the student shall send the student's school student record to the receiving school district.

(c) In the case of a transfer between school districts of a student who is eligible for special education and related services, when the parent or guardian of the student presents a copy of the student's then current Individualized Education Program (IEP) to the new school, the student shall be placed in a special education program in accordance with that described in the student's IEP.

(d) Until June 30, 2015, out-of-state transfer students, including children of military personnel that transfer into this State, may use unofficial transcripts for admission to a school until official transcripts are obtained from his or her last school district.

10/9. Actions; violations

(a) Any person aggrieved by any violation of this Act may institute an action for injunctive relief in the Circuit Court of the County in which the violation has occurred or the Circuit Court of the County in which the school is located.

(b) Any person injured by a willful or negligent violation of this Act may institute an action for damages in the Circuit Court of the County in which the violation has occurred or the Circuit Court of the County in which the school is located.

(c) In the case of any successful action under paragraph (a) or (b) of this Section, any person or school found to have willfully or negligently violated any provision of this Act is liable to the plaintiff for the plaintiff's damages, the costs of the action and reasonable attorneys' fees, as determined by the Court.

(d) Actions for injunctive relief to secure compliance with this Act may be brought by the State Board, by the State's Attorney of the County in which the alleged violation has occurred or the State's Attorney of the County in which the school is located, in each case in the Circuit Court of such County.

(e) Willful failure to comply with any Section of this Act is a petty offense; except that any person who willfully and maliciously falsifies any school student record, student permanent record or student temporary record shall be guilty of a Class A misdemeanor.

(f) Absent proof of malice, no cause of action or claim for relief, civil or criminal, may be maintained against any school, or employee or official of a school or person acting at the direction of a school for any statement made or judgment expressed in any entry to a school student record of a type which does not violate this Act or the regulations issued by the State Board pursuant to this Act; provided that this paragraph (f) does not limit or deny any defense available under existing law.

10/10. Severability

If any provision of this Act or the application thereof to any person or circumstance is held invalid, such invalidity does not affect other provisions or applications of the Act which can be given effect without the invalid provision or application, and to this end the provisions of this Act are declared to be severable.

Chapter 5

Managing Student Medical Needs and Medications

"He is the best physician that knows the worthlessness of most medicines."
— Benjamin Franklin

> **In This Chapter:**
>
> 5.1 Student Medication in General
> 5.2 The Role of Support Staff in Handing Student Medical Needs
> 5.3 Administration of Medication at School
> 5.4 Prescription v. Non-Prescription Medication
> 5.5 Self-Administration of Medication by Students
> 5.6 Diabetic Students
> 5.7 Emergency Medical Aid to Students
> 5.8 Storage and Maintenance of Medication
> 5.9 Notification to Parents and Students
> 5.10 Student Record Entries
>
> FAQs
> Checklists and Sample Forms
> References

5.1 Student Medication in General

The Illinois School Code provides that the administration of medication to students during regular school hours and during school-related activities should be discouraged unless absolutely necessary for the critical health and wellbeing of the student. However, the definition of absolutely necessary appears to be fairly broad, as parents request that schools administer prescription and non-prescription medication to students for a wide variety of illnesses and ailments.

Each school district is required to adopt a policy concerning the administration of medication to students. You should review your school district's medication policy in addition to the information in this chapter.

5.2 The Role of Support Staff in Handling Student Medical Needs

Support staff members are often called upon to administer medicine and medical treatment to students in the absence of a school nurse or administrator. These duties often include bandaging a cut, applying ice to a bump, handing out prescription medication and other things that are more serious in nature.

It is important to note that support staff employees cannot be forced to handle medication or administer medication to students. Only school administrators and nurses can be required to perform these tasks. Other school personnel may volunteer to administer or supervise the administration of student medication, but cannot be required to do so. In cases where a staff member agrees to assist with student medical needs, the employee should only perform those tasks for which he or she has received instruction and proper training.

Every school employee, however, has an affirmative obligation to assist students in the case of a medical emergency. Therefore, it is strongly recommended that all school employees participate in a basic first aid training course and complete CPR training. Additionally, it is important to be aware of the school district's policies and procedures on blood borne pathogens.

5.3 Administration of Medication at School

Students who need to take medication at school must have both written doctor and parent authorization. The doctor's authorization should include:

- The student's name and date of birth
- Name of the medication
- The reason the student takes the medication
- Intended effects of the medication and potential side effects
- A list of other medications that the student is taking
- The proper dosage
- Times the medication needs to be taken
- Instructions for administering the medication, including authorization for self-administration
- The prescriber's name, signature and contact information

All medication must be brought to school in its original, labeled container. Additionally, each dose of medication given to a student must be documented. For a sample log used to document the administration of medication to students, see sample Form 5-2.

5.4 Prescription v. Non-Prescription Medication

It is important to point out that ALL medication taken while at school MUST be done in accordance with the school's policies. This applies to prescription and non-prescription medication. Students who need to take non-prescription medication on a consistent, ongoing basis while at school must have the same doctor and parent authorization that is required for prescription medication. Additionally, non-prescription medication must be brought to school in the manufacturer's original packaging. It is also important to document the administration of non-prescription medication to students.

Sometimes students do not need to take medication on an ongoing basis, but simply come down to the school office and ask for an aspirin, cough drop or other temporary relief. School personnel should NEVER dispense these types of medications to students, even if the school employee knows the student or knows the student's parent. In such cases, the student must be referred to the school nurse or school administrator.

5.5 Self-Administration of Medication by Students

A school district may, by board policy, adopt guidelines allowing students to self-administer medication. You should consult your school district's policy regarding this issue.

State law, however, provides three medical conditions where students must (with proper authorization) be allowed to carry and self-administer their medication. These medications and underlying conditions are: (1) asthma inhalers for asthmatic students; (2) Epinephrine auto-injectors for students with allergies; and (3) diabetic testing supplies and insulin for diabetic students. Students of all ages who meet certain requirements must be allowed to carry and self-administer their medications. For a complete list and analysis of student self-administration of medication, see Checklist 5-1.

State law also exempts school districts and school employees from any liability with respect to students who carry and self-administer the above medications, except for cases where a school employee engages in willful and wanton conduct (meaning actual or deliberate intention to cause harm or utter indifference or conscious disregard).

5.6 Diabetic Students

In 2011, the Illinois State Legislature passed the Care of Students with Diabetes Act. In addition to allowing for students to carry and self-administer diabetic medications, this new law mandates that students with diabetic needs have a Diabetes Care Plan. This plan is generally developed by the student's parent and doctor and submitted to the school. Additionally, the new law provides that if a school has any student with diabetes, all school employees must receive training in the basics of diabetes care, how to identify when a student with diabetes needs immediate or emergency medical attention and whom to contact in the case of an emergency.

5.7 Emergency Medical Aid to Students

The Illinois School Code specifically provides that school employees who provide emergency medical assistance to students can do so without fear of liability. As long as emergency medical assistance is provided in a reasonable fashion, school officials are immune from any potential liability.

5.8 Storage and Maintenance of Medication

Student medication should be stored in a secured (locked) location and kept separate from other items. Medication requiring refrigeration should also be stored in a secured refrigerator and kept apart from other refrigerated food products.

5.9 Notification to Parents and Students

The school district's medication policy must be provided to a student's parent or guardian within 15 days of the beginning of the school year or within 15 days of the student beginning school in the district. Students must also be informed about the contents of the school district's medication policy.

5.10 Student Record Entries

Each dose of medication administered to a student must be documented in the daily medication administration log. This log is considered part of a student's temporary record.

Documentation must include the date, time, dosage, route by which the medication was administered and the signature of the person administering the medication or supervising the student in self-administration. In the event a dose of medication is not administered as ordered, the reasons must be entered in this record. See sample Form 5-2 for an example of how the administration of student medication must be documented.

FAQs

Can a school employee be required to give medication to a student?
School secretaries, teachers and other non-administrative school personnel cannot be required to dispense or administer medication to students. However, any school employee may volunteer to perform these functions with respect to student medication.

If I decide to assist with student medication, is there any special training that I need to receive?
It is strongly recommended that school employees receive instructions from the school nurse when agreeing to assist with student medication. Additionally, it is strongly recommended that all school staff take a course in basic first aid and CPR.

Can I be disciplined for refusing to assist a student with medical needs?
No. School officials cannot discipline an employee for refusing to assist with student medical needs. However, a school employee is generally obligated to assist a student in emergency circumstances where the student's health is in jeopardy.

Am I responsible if a student becomes ill after taking medication that I dispense?
As long as all procedures are properly followed, a school employee cannot generally be held liable if a student becomes ill after taking his or her medication. In the event of a lawsuit, the school district is required to provide the school employee with an attorney and pay all costs, including any judgment.

What should be done if medication is given to a student in error?
Whenever medication is given in error, school administration, the student's parent or guardian and medical personnel should be immediately contacted.

Can a student carry and self-administer his or her own medication?
You should consult your board's policy on this matter. However, Illinois law states that students must be allowed to possess and self-administer at their discretion asthma inhalers, Epinephrine auto-injectors and insulin and diabetic testing supplies. For more information, see Section 5.5 and Checklist 5-1.

Is it okay for a student to administer his or her own medication as long as I am supervising the student?
As long as the student's parent and physician acknowledge the student's ability to administer his or her own medication, this is generally acceptable, provided that the student is adequately supervised.

Are students allowed to possess and take aspirin and other non-prescription medication while at school?
Students may not possess and take non-prescription medication at school. Students who need to take non-prescription medication while at school must do so in accordance with the district's medication policy. This includes having the medication kept in the nurse's office or school office and having parent permission and doctor authorization.

Without parent consent, can I give a student an aspirin, cough drop or other non-prescription medication for temporary relief?

School employees should NEVER dispense these types of medications to students, even if the employee knows the student or knows the student's parent. In these cases, the student must be referred to the school nurse or school administrator.

Where does a school keep documentation of student medical issues and needs?

Student medical documentation must be maintained in the student's temporary file. For additional information, see Section 5.10.

Checklists and Sample Forms

Sample forms available at www.edlawyer.org

Checklist 5-1: Requirements for Student Self-Administration of Medication
(The chart below summarizes self-medication requirements for allergies, asthma and diabetes.)

Medical Condition	Allergies	Asthma	Diabetes
Students Can Carry and Self-Administer	Epinephrine auto-injector (EpiPen©)	Asthma Inhaler	Diabetic testing supplies and insulin
Parent Permission Required?	Parent permission required	Written authorization from parent required	Diabetic Care Plan signed by student's parent required
Doctor Permission Required?	Written authorization from physician, physician's assistant or advanced practice registered nurse required	None required	Health care provider instructions required, including copy of the prescription and methods of insulin administration
Additional Requirements	A written statement from physician, physician or advanced practice registered nurse containing name of medication and purpose, prescribed dosage and time or circumstances in which medication is to be administered	Parent must provide prescription containing name of medication, prescribed dosage and time or circumstances in which medication is to be administered	Diabetic Care Management Plan must serve as the basis for the student's 504 Plan
Liability	No liability, except for willful and wanton misconduct. Must inform parents in writing of liability waiver	No liability, except for willful and wanton misconduct. Must inform parents in writing of liability waiver	No liability, except for willful and wanton misconduct
Documentation to be Maintained by School	The information provided must be kept on file	The information provided must be kept on file	Diabetic Care Management Plan must be maintained by the school
Renewal	Authorization must be renewed each school year	Authorization must be renewed each school year	Yearly or sooner if the student's needs change

Managing Student Medical Needs and Medications   Illinois Law in the School Office

Sample Form 5-1: Sample Authorization and Permission for Administration of Medication

To be completed by the child's parent(s)/guardian(s). A new form must be completed every school year. Keep in the school nurse's office or, in the absence of a school nurse, the Building Principal's office.

Student Medical Authorization Form

(Required when a student needs to take prescription and non-prescription medication to be taken at school.)

Student's Name:_____ Birth Date: _____
Address: _____
Home Phone:_____Emergency Phone: _____
School:_____Grade:_____Teacher: _____

To be completed by the student's physician, physician assistant, or advanced practice RN (Note: for asthma inhalers only, use the "Asthma Inhalers" section below):

Physician's Printed Name: _____
Office Address: _____
Office Phone:_____Emergency Phone:_____
Medication name:_____
Purpose: _____
Dosage:_____Frequency:_____
Time medication is to be administered or under what circumstances: _____
Prescription date:_____Order date:_____Discontinuation date:_____
Diagnosis requiring medication: _____
Is it necessary for this medication to be administered during the school day? ___ Yes __ No
Expected side effects, if any: _____
Time interval for re-evaluation: _____
Other medications student is receiving:_____

_____
Physician's signature   Date _____

Asthma Inhalers
Parent(s)/Guardian(s) please attach prescription label here:

For only parents/guardians of students who need to carry asthma medication or an epinephrine auto-injector:

I authorize the School District and its employees and agents, to allow my child or ward to carry and self-administer his or her asthma inhaler and/or use his or her epinephrine auto-injector: (1) while in school, (2) while at a school-sponsored activity, (3) while under the supervision of school personnel, or (4) before or after normal school activities, such as while in before-school or after-school care on school-operated property. Illinois law requires the School District to inform parent(s)/guardian(s) that it, and its employees and agents, incur no liability, except for willful and wanton conduct, as a result of any injury arising from a student's self-administration of medication or epinephrine auto-injector (105 ILCS 5/22-30). **If you agree please initial:** _____

_____
Parent/Guardian

For all parents/guardians:
By signing below, I agree that I am primarily responsible for administering medication to my child. However, in the event that I am unable to do so or in the event of a medical emergency, I hereby authorize the School District and its employees and agents, in my behalf, to administer or to attempt to administer to my child (or to allow my child to self-administer pursuant to State law, while under the supervision of the employees and agents of the School District), lawfully prescribed medication in the manner described above. **I acknowledge that it may be necessary for the administration of medications to my child to be performed by an individual other than a school nurse and specifically consent to such practices**, and I agree to indemnify and hold harmless the School District and its employees and agents against any claims, except a claim based on willful and wanton conduct, arising out of the administration or the child's self-administration of medication.

_____
Parent/Guardian printed name
Address (if different from Student's above): _____
Phone:_____Emergency Phone: _____

_____   _____
Parent/Guardian signature   Date

Parent Authorization:

I hereby acknowledge that I am primarily responsible for administering medication to my child. However, in the event that I am unable to do so or in the event of a medical emergency, I hereby authorize (name of School District) and its employees and agents, on my behalf and stead, to administer or to attempt to administer to my child or to allow my child to self-administer while under the supervision of an employee or agent of the School District, lawfully prescribed medication in the manner described above. I acknowledge that it may be necessary for the administration of medication to my child to be performed by an individual other than a school nurse and I specifically consent to such practices. I further acknowledge and agree that when lawfully prescribed medication is so administered or attempted to be administered, I waive any claims that I might have against the School District, its employees and agents arising out of the administration of said medication. In addition I agree to hold harmless and indemnify the School Districts, its employees and agents, either jointly or severally, from and against any and all claims, damages, causes of action or injuries incurred or resulting from the administration or attempts at administration of said medication.

_____   _____
Parent's Signature   Date Signed

_____   _____
Parent's Phone Number   Parent's Emergency Phone Number

Additional Information:
_____
_____

Used with Permission from Illinois Association of School Boards, PRESS Form 7:270,E (10/10)

Sample Form 5-2: Sample Daily Medication Administration Record

Student: _____ Date of Birth: _____ School Year _____

Teacher: _____ Diagnosis: _____
Medication: _____
Date & Time: _____ Dosage: _____
Parent's Name & Emergency Phone Number: _____
Physician's Name & Contact Information: _____

Code or Initial the Appropriate Box

	1	2	3	4	5	6	7	8	9	10	11	12	13	14	15	16	17	18	19	20	21	22	23	24	25	26	27	28	29	30	31
Aug																															
Sept																															
Oct																															
Nov																															
Dec																															
Jan																															
Feb																															
Mar																															
Apr																															
May																															
June																															
July																															

Name   Initials   Codes
_____ _____ H: Holiday or Weekend   F: Field Trip
_____ _____ A: Student Absent   D: Early Dismissal
_____ _____ N: No Medication Available   W: Dose Withheld
_____ _____ O: Student No Show

Sample Form 5-3: Sample Certificate of Physical Fitness for Participation in Athletics

<u>Certificate of Physical Fitness for Participation in Athletics</u>

To be submitted to the Building Principal. (please print)
Student _____ Sport/Activity _____
Parent/Guardian _____ Home phone _____
Home address _____ Cell phone _____
Emergency contact *(relationship to student)* _____ Contact phone _____
Physician _____ Physician phone
Medical History: Date of Birth: _____ Height: _____ Weight _____

❏ Heart condition   ❏ Diabetes   ❏ Asthma: ❏ Requires student to carry EpiPen®
❏ Epilepsy   ❏ Allergies: ❏ Requires child to self-administer medication
❏ Other _____

List all medications *(prescribed and over the counter)*
_____

Injuries *(brief description and dates)*
_____

Surgeries *(brief description and dates)*
_____

Physical activity restrictions (brief description and duration)

I certify that:

1. My child is in good health and is capable of participating in the above sport or activity. No need exists to limit his/her participation. I assume full responsibility for his/her physical condition and participation, and will notify you of any changes.

2. I have completed and submitted the *Authorization for Medical Treatment* form allowing the school to seek medical treatment for my child in the event of a medical emergency when reasonable attempts to contact me are unsuccessful.

3. If my child requires or may need medication while participating in athletics, I have completed and submitted the *School Medication Authorization Form*.

Parent/Guardian signature_____ Date _____

Used with Permission from Illinois Association of School Boards, PRESS Form 7:300,E2
(02/08)

Sample Form 5-4: Sample Authorization for Medical Treatment

<u>Authorization for Medical Treatment</u>
To be submitted to the Superintendent. (please print)

Student _____ Sport/Activity _____
Parent/Guardian_____ Home phone _____
Home address_____ Cell phone _____
Physician _____ Physician phone _____
Medical Information: *(list allergies, medications, conditions and any known restrictions)*
_____
_____
_____
_____
_____

    In the event of a medical emergency and if reasonable attempts to contact me using the telephone numbers listed above are unsuccessful:

    I, as parent or legal guardian of the above student, do hereby authorize:

1. Treatment by a licensed medical physician of my child/ward in the event of a medical emergency that, in the opinion of the attending physician, may endanger his/her life, cause disfigurement, physical impairment, or undue discomfort if delayed, and

2. Transfer of my child/ward to any hospital reasonably accessible at my expense.

Parent/Guardian signature_____ Date _____

Used with Permission from Illinois Association of School Boards, PRESS Form 7:300, E3
(02/08)

References

105 ILCS 5/10-20.14b. Medication Policy.
To develop a policy for administration of medications in schools, to furnish a copy of the policy to the parents or guardians of each pupil within 15 days after the beginning of each school year, or within 15 days after starting classes for a pupil who transfers into the district, and to require that each school informs its pupils of the contents of its policy.

105 ILCS 5/10-22.21b. Administering Medication.
To provide for the administration of medication to students. It shall be the policy of the State of Illinois that the administration of medication to students during regular school hours and during school-related activities should be discouraged unless absolutely necessary for the critical health and well-being of the student. Under no circumstances shall teachers or other non-administrative school employees, except certified school nurses and non-certificated registered professional nurses, be required to administer medication to students. This Section shall not prohibit a school district from adopting guidelines for self-administration of medication by students. This Section shall not prohibit any school employee from providing emergency assistance to students.

105 ILCS 5/22-30. Self-Administration of Medication.
(a) In this Section:
"Asthma inhaler" means a quick reliever asthma inhaler.
"Epinephrine auto-injector" means a medical device for immediate self-administration by a person at risk of anaphylaxis.
"Medication" means a medicine, prescribed by (i) a physician licensed to practice medicine in all its branches, (ii) a physician assistant who has been delegated the authority to prescribe asthma medications by his or her supervising physician, or (iii) an advanced practice registered nurse who has a written collaborative agreement with a collaborating physician that delegates the authority to prescribe asthma medications, for a pupil that pertains to the pupil's asthma and that has an individual prescription label.
"Self-administration" means a pupil's discretionary use of and ability to carry his or her prescribed asthma medication.

(b) A school, whether public or nonpublic, must permit the self-administration of medication by a pupil with asthma or the use of an epinephrine auto-injector by a pupil, provided that:

  (1) the parents or guardians of the pupil provide to the school (i) written authorization from the parents or guardians for the self-administration of medication or (ii) for use of an epinephrine auto-injector, written authorization from the pupil's physician, physician assistant, or advanced practice registered nurse; and

  (2) the parents or guardians of the pupil provide to the school (i) the prescription label, which must contain the name of the medication, the prescribed dosage, and the time at which or circumstances under which the medication is to be adminis-

tered, or (ii) for use of an epinephrine auto-injector, a written statement from the pupil's physician, physician assistant, or advanced practice registered nurse containing the following information:

(A) the name and purpose of the epinephrine auto-injector;

(B) the prescribed dosage; and

(C) the time or times at which or the special circumstances under which the epinephrine auto-injector is to be administered.

The information provided shall be kept on file in the office of the school nurse or, in the absence of a school nurse, the school's administrator.

(b-5) A school district or nonpublic school may authorize the provision of an epinephrine auto-injector to a student or any personnel authorized under a student's Individual Health Care Action Plan, Illinois Food Allergy Emergency Action Plan and Treatment Authorization Form, or plan pursuant to Section 504 of the Federal Rehabilitation Act of 1973 to administer an epinephrine auto-injector to the student, that meets the prescription on file.

(b-10) The school district or nonpublic school may authorize a school nurse do the following: (i) provide an epinephrine auto-injector to a student or any personnel authorized under a student's Individual Health Care Action Plan, Illinois Food Allergy Emergency Action Plan and Treatment Authorization Form, or plan pursuant to Section 504 of the Federal Rehabilitation Act of 1973 to administer an epinephrine auto-injector to the student, that meets the prescription on file; (ii) administer an epinephrine auto-injector that meets the prescription on file to any student who has an Individual Health Care Action Plan, Illinois Food Allergy Emergency Action Plan and Treatment Authorization Form, or plan pursuant to Section 504 of the Federal Rehabilitation Act of 1973 that authorizes the use of an Epinephrine auto-injector; and (iii) administer an epinephrine auto-injector to any student that the school nurse in good faith professionally believes is having an anaphylactic reaction.

(c) The school district or nonpublic school must inform the parents or guardians of the pupil, in writing, that the school district or nonpublic school and its employees and agents, including a physician providing standing protocol or prescription for school epinephrine auto-injectors, are to incur no liability, except for willful and wanton conduct, as a result of any injury arising from the self-administration of medication or use of an epinephrine auto-injector regardless of whether authorization was given by the pupil's parents or guardians or by the pupil's physician, physician's assistant, or advanced practice registered nurse. The parents or guardians of the pupil must sign a statement acknowledging that the school district or nonpublic school and its employees and agents are to incur no liability, except for willful and wanton conduct, as a result of any injury arising from the self-administration of medication or use of an epinephrine auto-injector regardless of whether authorization was given by the pupil's parents or guardians or by the pupil's physician, physician's assistant, or advanced practice registered nurse and that the parents or guardians must indemnify and hold harmless the school district or nonpublic school and its employees and agents against any claims, except a claim based on willful and wanton conduct, arising out of the self-administration of medication or use of an epinephrine auto-injector regardless of whether authorization was given by the pupil's parents or guardians or by the pupil's physician, physician's assistant, or advanced practice registered nurse. When a school nurse administers an epinephrine auto-injector to a student whom the school nurse in good faith professionally believes is having an anaphylactic reaction, notwithstanding the lack of notice to the parents or guardians of the pupil or the absence of the parents or guardians signed statement acknowledging no liability, except for willful and wanton conduct, the school district or nonpublic school and its employees and agents, including a physician providing standing protocol or prescription for school epinephrine auto-injectors, are to incur no liability, except for willful and wanton conduct, as a result of any injury arising from the use of an epinephrine auto-injector regardless of whether authorization was given by the pupil's parents or guardians or by the pupil's physician, physician's assistant, or advanced practice registered nurse.

(d) The permission for self-administration of medication or use of an epinephrine auto-injector is effective for the school year for which it is granted and shall be renewed each subsequent school year upon fulfillment of the requirements of this Section.

(e) Provided that the requirements of this Section are fulfilled, a pupil with asthma may possess and use his or her medication or a pupil may possess and use an epinephrine auto-injector (i) while in school, (ii) while at a school-sponsored activity, (iii) while under the supervision of school personnel, or (iv) before or after normal school activities, such as while in before-school or after-school care on school-operated property.

(f) The school district or nonpublic school may maintain at a school in a locked, secure location a supply of epinephrine auto-injectors. A physician may prescribe epinephrine auto-injectors in the name of the school district or nonpublic school to be maintained for use when necessary. The school district or nonpublic school supply of epinephrine auto-injectors may be provided to and utilized by any student authorized to self-administer that meets the prescription on file or by any personnel authorized under a student's Individual Health Care Action Plan, Illinois Food Allergy Emergency Action Plan and Treatment Authorization Form, or plan pursuant to Section 504 of the federal Rehabilitation Act of 1973 to administer an epinephrine auto-injector to the student, that meets the prescription on file. When a student does not have an epinephrine auto-injector or a prescription for an epinephrine auto-injector on file, the school nurse may utilize the school district or nonpublic school supply of epinephrine auto-injectors to respond to anaphylactic reaction, under a standing protocol from a physician licensed to practice medicine in all its branches and the requirements of this Section.

105 ILCS 145/15, et. seq. Care of Students with Diabetes Act.

§ 1. Short title. This Act may be cited as the Care of Students with Diabetes Act.

§ 5. Legislative findings. The General Assembly finds the following:

(1) Diabetes is a serious chronic disease in which the pancreas does not make insulin (Type 1) or the body cannot use insulin properly (Type 2).

(2) Diabetes must be managed 24 hours a day to avoid the potentially life-threatening, short-term consequences of low blood sugar and prevent or delay the serious

(3) Federal law affords people with diabetes specific rights and protections. These laws include Section 504 of the Rehabilitation Act of 1973, the Individuals with Disabilities Education Improvement Act of 2004, and the Americans with Disabilities Act of 1990, and the ADA Amendments Act of 2008.

(4) Federal laws enforced consistently in schools provide students with diabetes equal educational opportunities and a healthy and safe environment.

(5) A school nurse is the most appropriate person in a school setting to provide for all students' healthcare needs; however, a school nurse may not be available when needed, and many schools do not have a full-time nurse.

(6) Many students are capable of checking their blood glucose levels, calculating a carbohydrate-to-insulin ratio, and administering insulin independently. Allowing capable students to manage diabetes independently in school is consistent with the recommendations of pediatric endocrinologists and certified diabetes educators and other specialists.

(7) Because appropriate and consistent diabetes care decreases the risks of serious short-term and long-term complications, increases a student's learning opportunities, and promotes individual and public health benefits, the General Assembly deems it in the public interest to enact this Act.

§ 10. Definitions. As used in this Act:

"Delegated care aide" means a school employee who has agreed to receive training in diabetes care and to assist students in implementing their diabetes care plan and has entered into an agreement with a parent or guardian and the school district or private school.

"Diabetes care plan" means a document that specifies the diabetes-related services needed by a student at school and at school-sponsored activities and identifies the appropriate staff to provide and supervise these services.

"Health care provider" means a physician licensed to practice medicine in all of its branches, advanced practice nurse who has a written agreement with a collaborating physician who authorizes the provision of diabetes care, or a physician assistant who has a written supervision agreement with a supervising physician who authorizes the provision of diabetes care.

"Principal" means the principal of the school.

"School" means any primary or secondary public, charter, or private school located in this State.

"School employee" means a person who is employed by a public school district or private school, a person who is employed by a local health department and assigned to a school, or a person who contracts with a school or school district to perform services in connection with a student's diabetes care plan. This definition must not be interpreted as requiring a school district or private school to hire additional personnel for the sole purpose of serving as a designated care aide.

§ 15. Diabetes care plan.

(a) A diabetes care plan shall serve as the basis of a student's Section 504 plan and shall be signed by a student's parent or guardian and submitted to the school for any student with diabetes who seeks assistance with diabetes care in the school setting, unless the student has been managing his or her diabetes care in the school setting before the effective date of this Act, in which case the student's parent or guardian may sign and submit a diabetes care plan under this Act. It is the responsibility of the student's parent or guardian to share the health care provider's instructions concerning the student's diabetes management during the school day. The diabetes care plan shall include the treating health care provider's instructions concerning the student's diabetes management during the school day, including a copy of the signed prescription and the methods of insulin administration.

(b) The services and accommodations specified in a diabetes care plan shall be reasonable, reflect the current standard of diabetes care, include appropriate safeguards to ensure that syringes and lancets are disposed of properly, and include requirements for diet, glucose testing, insulin administration, and treatment for hypoglycemia, hyperglycemia, and emergency situations.

(c) A diabetes care plan shall include a uniform record of glucometer readings and insulin administered by the school nurse or delegated care aide during the school day using a standardized format provided by the State Board of Education.

(d) A diabetes care plan shall include procedures regarding when a delegated care aide shall consult with the parent or guardian, school nurse, where available, or health care provider to confirm that an insulin dosage is appropriate.

(e) A diabetes care plan shall be submitted to the school at the beginning of the school year; upon enrollment, as soon as practical following a student's diagnosis; or when a student's care needs change during the school year. Parents shall be responsible for informing the school in a timely manner of any changes to the diabetes care plan and their emergency contact numbers.

§ 20. Delegated care aides.

(a) Delegated care aides shall perform the duties necessary to assist a student with diabetes in accordance with his or her diabetes care plan and in compliance with any guidelines provided during training under Section 25 of this Act.

(b) In accordance with the diabetes care plan or when an unexpected snack or meal requires a dose of insulin not anticipated by a student's diabetes care plan, the delegated care aide shall consult with the parent or guardian, school nurse, where available, or health care provider to confirm that the insulin dosage is appropriate given the number of carbohydrates to be taken and the student's blood glucose level as determined by a glucometer reading.

(c) The principal shall facilitate compliance with the provisions of a diabetes care plan.

(d) Delegated care aides are authorized to provide assistance by a student's parents or guardian and the school district or private school.

§ 25. Training for school employees and delegated care aides.

(a) In schools that have a student with diabetes, all school employees shall receive training in the basics of diabetes care, how to identify when a student with diabetes needs immediate or emergency medical attention, and whom to contact in the case of an emergency during regular inservice training under Section 3-11 of the School Code.

(b) Delegated care aides shall be trained to perform the tasks necessary to assist a student with diabetes in accordance with his or her diabetes care plan, including training to do the following:

  (1) check blood glucose and record results;

  (2) recognize and respond to the symptoms of hypoglycemia according to the diabetes care plan;

  (3) recognize and respond to the symptoms of hyperglycemia according to the diabetes care plan;

  (4) estimate the number of carbohydrates in a snack or lunch;

  (5) administer insulin according to the student's diabetes care plan and keep a record of the amount administered; and

  (6) respond in an emergency, including how to administer glucagon and call 911.

(c) The school district shall coordinate staff training.

(d) Initial training of a delegated care aide shall be provided by a licensed healthcare provider with expertise in diabetes or a certified diabetic educator and individualized by a student's parent or guardian. Training must be consistent with the guidelines provided by the U.S. Department of Health and Human Services in the guide for school personnel entitled "Helping the Student with Diabetes Succeed". The training shall be updated when the diabetes care plan is changed and at least annually.

(e) School nurses, where available, or health care providers may provide technical assistance or consultation or both to delegated care aides.

(f) An information sheet shall be provided to any school employee who transports a student for school-sponsored activities. It shall identify the student with diabetes, identify potential emergencies that may occur as a result of the student's diabetes and the appropriate responses to such emergencies, and provide emergency contact information.

§ 30. Self-management. Provided that the student is authorized according to his or her diabetes care plan, a student shall be permitted to do the following:

  (1) check blood glucose when and wherever needed;

  (2) administer insulin with the insulin delivery system used by the student;

  (3) treat hypoglycemia and hyperglycemia and otherwise attend to the care and management of his or her diabetes in the classroom, in any area of the school or school grounds and at any school-related activity or event in accordance with the diabetes care plan; and

  (4) possess on his or her person, at all times, the supplies and equipment necessary to monitor and treat diabetes, including, but not limited to, glucometers, lancets, test

strips, insulin, syringes, insulin pens and needle tips, insulin pumps, infusion sets, alcohol swabs, a glucagon injection kit, glucose tablets, and food and drink, in accordance with the diabetes care plan.

§ 35. Restricting access to school prohibited. A school district shall not restrict the assignment of a student with diabetes to a particular school on the basis that the school does not have a full-time school nurse, nor shall a school deny a student access to any school or school-related activities on the basis that a student has diabetes.

§ 40. Protections against retaliation. A school employee shall not be subject to any penalty, sanction, reprimand, discharge, demotion, denial of a promotion, withdrawal of benefits, or other disciplinary action for choosing not to agree to serve as a delegated care aide.

§ 45. Civil immunity.
(a) A school or a school employee is not liable for civil or other damages as a result of conduct, other than willful or wanton misconduct, related to the care of a student with diabetes.
(b) A school employee shall not be subject to any disciplinary proceeding resulting from an action taken in compliance with this Act, unless the action constitutes willful or wanton misconduct.

§ 50. Federal law. Nothing in this Act shall limit any rights available under federal law.

Chapter 6

Immunization, Health, Dental and Vision Requirements

"I pictured myself as a virus or cancer cell and tried to sense what it would be like."
– Jonas Salk

In This Chapter:

- 6.1 Introduction
- 6.2 Health Examination Requirements
- 6.3 Required Immunizations
- 6.4 Dental Examinations
- 6.5 Eye Examinations
- 6.6 Exemptions and Waivers
- 6.7 Homeless Students

FAQs
Checklists and Sample Forms
References

6.1 Introduction

Students are required to have health, dental and vision exams and proof of immunization at various points in their education. The sections below and Checklist 6-1 provide details on timelines, penalties for non-compliance and the ability of parents to seek a waiver from compliance.

6.2 Health Examination Requirements

A health exam is required before a child:
- Enters Kindergarten or first grade
- Enters sixth grade
- Enters ninth grade
- Enrolls in an Illinois school for the first time, regardless of the student's grade

A diabetes screening must be included as part of each health exam, though a diabetes test is not required. Children age six and under must provide as part of the health exam a statement that the child was "risk-assessed" or screened for lead poisoning. Additionally, female students entering sixth grade are encouraged to consider a human papilloma vaccine (HPV).

The health exam must be reported on the Certificate of Child Health Examination form. (For a copy, see sample Form 6-1.) The exam must also be performed by a physician licensed to practice medicine in all of its branches, an advanced practice nurse who has a written collaborative agreement with a physician or a physician assistant who has been delegated the performance of health examinations by his or her supervising physician. Note that if a registered nurse performs any part of a health exam, then a physician must review and sign all required report forms.

In order for the exam to be current, it must have been completed within one year of the first day of school. If a child does not submit proof of compliance by October 15 (or by an earlier date established by the school district), the child must be excluded from school until such time as the child's health exam is up-to-date or the child's parent claims a religious exemption.

6.3 Required Immunizations

Proof of immunization is required at the same time as the health exam. A child must be excluded from school if he or she does not have proper immunizations by October 15 (or an earlier date established by the school district.) The exclusion from school must continue until the child shows proof of immunizations or claims a waiver. A waiver must be accepted if the parent has a medical objection or objection based on religious beliefs.

Until June 30, 2015, if the student is an out-of-state transfer student and does not have proof of the required immunizations, then the student may only attend classes if he or she has proof that an appointment for the required vaccinations has been scheduled. If proof is not submitted within 30 days, then the student must be removed from school until the vaccinations have been performed.

6.4 Dental Examinations

Children entering Kindergarten, second and sixth grade must present proof of a dental exam performed by a licensed dentist before May 15 of the school year. The examination must have been performed within the prior 18 months in order for it to be current.

If a child fails to undergo the required dental exam, the school may withhold the child's report card until such time as the dental exam is completed or the child's parent presents proof that a dental exam will be completed within 60 days of the May 15 deadline.

Parents may also claim a waiver or exemption for religious reasons, lack of access to a provider or undue hardship. A school may not exclude a child from participation in school due to his or her failure to obtain a dental exam.

6.5 Eye Examinations

Parents are encouraged to have their child undergo an eye exam at the time of the required health physical. An eye exam is required for children entering Kindergarten or an Illinois school for the first time. The exam must be performed by a physician or optometrist. The exam must have been completed within the previous one year in order for it to be current. The eye exam must be presented to the school by October 15. If a student fails to undergo the required exam, a school may withhold the child's report card until such time as the eye exam is completed or the child's parent presents proof that the eye exam will be completed within 60 days of the October 15 deadline.

Parents may opt out of having their child take an eye exam based on lack of access to a provider, undue hardship or a religious objection. A school may not exclude a child from participation in school due to his or her failure to obtain an eye exam.

6.6 Exemptions and Waivers

Parents who object to immunizations, health, dental or eye exams on religious grounds are not required to comply if they provide to the school a signed statement that details the grounds for the objection.

If the child has a physical condition that precludes one or more of the required immunizations, the examining physician, advanced practice nurse or physician assistant responsible for the performance of the health exam must endorse this fact upon the health exam form.

A child may also be exempt from the eye exam and/or dental exam due to an undue burden or lack of access to a provider.

6.7 Homeless Students

State law requires that a homeless child must be immediately admitted to school, even if the child or child's parent is unable to produce immunization and health records that are otherwise required for enrollment.

FAQs

What is the deadline for a child showing proof of a health exam and immunizations?
October 15 of the school year, unless an earlier date is required by the school district.

Who is authorized to perform the health examination?
Physicians licensed to practice medicine in all of its branches, advanced practice nurses who have a written collaborative agreement with a physician or physician assistants who have been delegated the performance of health examinations by their supervising physician. If a registered nurse performs any part of a health examination, then a physician must review and sign all required report forms.

On the health examination form, is a physician's stamp instead of an actual signature acceptable?
Yes.

What is considered to be a current health examination?
The health exam must be completed within one year of the first day of school in order for it to be current.

What should be done if a child does not comply with the health examination and immunizations by October 15th?
If a child does not comply by October 15, or by the earlier date established by the school district, the child must be excluded from school until such time as the child presents proof of having had the health exam and required immunizations or claims a valid exemption for religious reasons.

Until June 30, 2015, if the student is an out-of-state transfer student and does not have proof of the required immunizations, then the student may only attend classes if he or she has proof that an appointment for the required vaccinations has been scheduled. If proof is not submitted within 30 days, then the student must be removed from school until the vaccinations have been performed.

Is lead screening required as part of the health examination?
Yes, for children six years of age and younger prior to entering Kindergarten or first grade.

Is a diabetes screening required as part of the health examination?
A diabetes screening must be included as part of each health exam, though a diabetes test is not required

Can the health examination form be used as a sports physical?
If the student is required to have a sports physical in the year that coincides with the child health examination requirement, the Certificate of Child Health Examination may be accepted as proof of examination for interscholastic sports if the statement regarding participation in interscholastic sports is completed by the health care provider.

Can a child's parent opt out from having the child immunized?
Yes, a waiver must be accepted if the parent has an objection based on religious beliefs.

What is the deadline for a child showing proof of a dental examination?
May 15 of the school year in which it is required.

Who can perform the dental examination?
Only a licensed dentist can perform the dental exam.

What is considered to be a current dental examination?
School dental exams must be completed within 18 months of the May 15 deadline in order to be considered current.

What can be done if a child does not comply with the dental examination as required?
If a child fails to undergo the required dental exam, the school may withhold the child's report card until such time as the dental exam is completed or the parent presents proof that the dental exam will be completed within 60 days of the May 15 deadline or claims a valid waiver or exemption.

Can a child's parent opt out from having the child receive a dental examination?
Yes, based on lack of access, undue burden or religious objection.

What is the deadline for a child showing proof of an eye examination?
October 15 of the school year in which it is required.

Who can perform the eye examination?
Either a physician or licensed optometrist can perform the eye exam.

What is considered to be a current eye examination?
The eye exam must be completed within one year of the first day of the school in order to be considered current.

What can be done if a child does not comply with the eye examination as required?
If a child fails to undergo the required eye exam, the school may withhold the child's report card until such time as the eye exam is completed or the parent presents proof that the eye exam will be completed within 60 days of the October 15 deadline or claims a valid waiver or exemption.

Can a child's parent opt out from having the child receive an eye examination?
Yes, based on lack of access, undue burden or religious objection.

Checklists and Sample Forms

Sample forms available at www.edlawyer.org

Checklist 6-1: Immunizations, Physical, Dental and Eye Exam Requirements

Requirements	Law	Compliance Date	Other Information	Waiver Provision	Consequences for Non-Compliance
Immunizations	At the time of the health exam, every child shall present proof of immunization	Required before October 15, unless an earlier date is established by the district	Basic Immunizations Diphtheria, Pertussis, Tetanus, polio, Measles, Rubella, Mumps, Haemophilus Influenzae type b, Hepatitis B and Varicella	Based on religious objection or medical objection	Must exclude from school until immunizations completed
Health Examination	Within one year of entering: an Illinois school for the first time, Kindergarten or first grade, sixth grade and ninth grade	Required before October 15, unless an earlier date is established by the district	Lead screening required for children age 6 and younger	Based on religious objection	Must exclude from school until exam has been completed
Dental Examination	All children in Kindergarten and the second and sixth grades	Required before May 15	Each school must give notice of this dental exam requirement to the parents and guardians of students at least 60 days before May 15 of each school year	Based on lack of access, undue burden or religious objection	May withhold the report card until exam done, proof of appointment within 60 days of May 15th, hardship waiver or religious objection
Eye Examination	All children entering Kindergarten or upon first entering an Illinois school	Required before October 15	Exams must have been completed within 12 months of the October 15 deadline	Based on lack of access, undue burden or religious objection	May withhold the report card until exam done, proof of appointment within 60 days of October 15th, hardship waiver or religious objection

Illinois Law in the School Office   Immunization, Health, Dental and Vision Requirements

Sample Form 6-1: Certificate of Child Health Examination

State of Illinois
Certificate of Child Health Examination

FOR USE IN DCFS LICENSED CHILD CARE FACILITIES
CFS 600
Rev 12/2011

Student's Name			Birth Date	Sex	Race/Ethnicity	School /Grade Level/ID#
Last	First	Middle	Month/Day/Year			
Address	Street	City	Zip Code	Parent/Guardian	Telephone # Home	Work

IMMUNIZATIONS: To be completed by health care provider. Note the mo/da/yr for *every* dose administered. The day and month is required if you cannot determine if the vaccine was given *after* the minimum interval or age. **If a specific vaccine is medically contraindicated, a separate written statement must be attached explaining the medical reason for the contraindication.**

Vaccine / Dose	1 MO DA YR	2 MO DA YR	3 MO DA YR	4 MO DA YR	5 MO DA YR	6 MO DA YR
DTP or **DTaP**						
Tdap; **Td** or Pediatric **DT** (Check specific type)	☐Tdap☐Td☐DT	☐Tdap☐Td☐DT	☐Tdap☐Td☐DT	☐Tdap☐Td☐DT	☐Tdap☐Td☐DT	☐Tdap☐Td☐DT
Polio (Check specific type)	☐ IPV ☐ OPV	☐ IPV ☐ OPV	☐ IPV ☐ OPV	☐ IPV ☐ OPV	☐ IPV ☐ OPV	☐ IPV ☐ OPV
Hib Haemophilus influenza type b						
Hepatitis B (HB)						
Varicella (Chickenpox)				COMMENTS:		
MMR Combined Measles Mumps. Rubella						
Single Antigen Vaccines	Measles		Rubella		Mumps	
Pneumococcal Conjugate						
Other/Specify Meningococcal, Hepatitis A, HPV, Influenza						

Health care provider (MD, DO, APN, PA, school health professional, health official) verifying above immunization history must sign below.   If adding dates to the above immunization history section, put your initials by date(s) and sign here.

Signature   Title   Date

Signature   Title   Date

ALTERNATIVE PROOF OF IMMUNITY
1. Clinical diagnosis is acceptable if verified by physician.   *(All measles cases diagnosed on or after July 1, 2002, must be confirmed by laboratory evidence.)

*MEASLES (Rubeola) MO DA YR   MUMPS MO DA YR   VARICELLA MO DA YR   Physician's Signature
2. History of varicella (chickenpox) disease is acceptable if verified by health care provider, school health professional or health official.
Person signing below is verifying that the parent/guardian's description of varicella disease history is indicative of past infection and is accepting such history as documentation of disease.

Date of Disease   Signature   Title   Date
3. Laboratory confirmation (check one) ☐Measles   ☐Mumps   ☐Rubella   ☐Hepatitis B   ☐Varicella
Lab Results   Date   MO   DA   YR   (Attach copy of lab result)

VISION AND HEARING SCREENING BY IDPH CERTIFIED SCREENING TECHNICIAN											
Date											Code:
Age/Grade											P = Pass
	R L	R L	R L	R L	R L	R L	R L	R L	R L	R L	F = Fail
Vision											U = Unable to test
Hearing											R = Referred G/C = Glasses/Contacts

IL444-4737 (R-01-12)   (COMPLETE BOTH SIDES)   Printed by Authority of the State of Illinois

Immunization, Health, Dental and Vision Requirements   Illinois Law in the School Office

Last	First	Middle	Birth Date Month/Day/Year	Sex	School	Grade Level/ ID

HEALTH HISTORY — TO BE COMPLETED AND SIGNED BY PARENT/GUARDIAN AND VERIFIED BY HEALTH CARE PROVIDER

ALLERGIES (Food, drug, insect, other)				MEDICATION (List all prescribed or taken on a regular basis.)			
Diagnosis of asthma?	Yes	No		Loss of function of one of paired organs? (eye/ear/kidney/testicle)	Yes	No	
Child wakes during night coughing?	Yes	No					
Birth defects?	Yes	No		Hospitalizations? When? What for?	Yes	No	
Developmental delay?	Yes	No					
Blood disorders? Hemophilia, Sickle Cell, Other? Explain.	Yes	No		Surgery? (List all.) When? What for?	Yes	No	
Diabetes?	Yes	No		Serious injury or illness?	Yes	No	
Head injury/Concussion/Passed out?	Yes	No		TB skin test positive (past/present)?	Yes*	No	*If yes, refer to local health department.
Seizures? What are they like?	Yes	No		TB disease (past or present)?	Yes*	No	
Heart problem/Shortness of breath?	Yes	No		Tobacco use (type, frequency)?	Yes	No	
Heart murmur/High blood pressure?	Yes	No		Alcohol/Drug use?	Yes	No	
Dizziness or chest pain with exercise?	Yes	No		Family history of sudden death before age 50? (Cause?)	Yes	No	
Eye/Vision problems? ___ ☐ Glasses ☐ Contacts ☐ Last exam by eye doctor ___				Dental ☐ Braces ☐ • Bridge ☐ • Plate Other			
Other concerns? (crossed eye, drooping lids, squinting, difficulty reading)							
Ear/Hearing problems?	Yes	No		Information may be shared with appropriate personnel for health and educational purposes. Parent/Guardian Signature Date			
Bone/Joint problem/injury/scoliosis?	Yes	No					

PHYSICAL EXAMINATION REQUIREMENTS   Entire section below to be completed by MD/DO/APN/PA
HEAD CIRCUMFERENCE if < 2-3 years old   HEIGHT   WEIGHT   BMI   B/P

DIABETES SCREENING (NOT REQUIRED FOR DAY CARE)   BMI>85% age/sex Yes☐ No☐   And any two of the following: **Family History** Yes ☐ No ☐   **Ethnic Minority** Yes ☐ No ☐   **Signs of Insulin Resistance** (hypertension, dyslipidemia, polycystic ovarian syndrome, acanthosis nigricans) Yes ☐ No ☐   **At Risk** Yes ☐ No ☐

LEAD RISK QUESTIONNAIRE Required for children age 6 months through 6 years enrolled in licensed or public school operated day care, preschool, nursery school and/or kindergarten.
Questionnaire Administered ? Yes ☐ No ☐   Blood Test Indicated? Yes ☐ No ☐   Blood Test Date _____ (Blood test required if resides in Chicago.)

TB SKIN OR BLOOD TEST Recommended only for children in high-risk groups including children immunosuppressed due to HIV infection or other conditions, frequent travel to or born in high prevalence countries or those exposed to adults in high-risk categories. See CDC guidelines.   No test needed ☐   Test performed ☐
  Skin Test: Date Read   __/__/__   Result: Positive ☐ Negative ☐   mm _____
  Blood Test: Date Reported __/__/__   Result: Positive ☐ Negative ☐   Value _____

LAB TESTS (Recommended)	Date	Results		Date	Results
Hemoglobin or Hematocrit			Sickle Cell (when indicated)		
Urinalysis			Developmental Screening Tool		

SYSTEM REVIEW	Normal	Comments/Follow-up/Needs		Normal	Comments/Follow-up/Needs
Skin			Endocrine		
Ears			Gastrointestinal		
Eyes		Amblyopia Yes☐ No☐	Genito-Urinary		LMP
Nose			Neurological		
Throat			Musculoskeletal		
Mouth/Dental			Spinal Exam		
Cardiovascular/HTN			Nutritional status		
Respiratory		☐ Diagnosis of Asthma	Mental Health		
Currently Prescribed Asthma Medication: ☐ Quick-relief medication (e.g. Short Acting Beta Antagonist) ☐ Controller medication (e.g. inhaled corticosteroid)			Other		

NEEDS/MODIFICATIONS required in the school setting   **DIETARY** Needs/Restrictions

SPECIAL INSTRUCTIONS/DEVICES e.g. safety glasses, glass eye, chest protector for arrhythmia, pacemaker, prosthetic device, dental bridge, false teeth, athletic support/cup

MENTAL HEALTH/OTHER   Is there anything else the school should know about this student?
If you would like to discuss this student's health with school or school health personnel, check title: ☐ Nurse   ☐ Teacher   ☐ Counselor   ☐ Principal

EMERGENCY ACTION needed while at school due to child's health condition (e.g. ,seizures, asthma, insect sting, food, peanut allergy, bleeding problem, diabetes, heart problem)?
Yes ☐   No ☐   If yes, please describe.

On the basis of the examination on this day, I approve this child's participation in   (If No or Modified please attach explanation.)
PHYSICAL EDUCATION   Yes ☐   No ☐   Modified ☐   **INTERSCHOLASTIC SPORTS** (for one year)   Yes ☐   No ☐   Limited ☐

Print Name   (MD,DO, APN, PA)   Signature   Date

Address   Phone

(Complete Both Sides)

Illinois State Board of Education (12/11)

Illinois Law in the School Office   Immunization, Health, Dental and Vision Requirements

Sample Form 6-2: Proof of School Dental Examination Form

State of Illinois
Illinois Department of Public Health

PROOF OF SCHOOL DENTAL EXAMINATION FORM

To be completed by the parent (please print):

Student's Name:	Last	First	Middle	Birth Date: (Month/Day/Year) / /
Address:	Street	City	ZIP Code	Telephone:
Name of School:			Grade Level:	Gender: ☐ Male ☐ Female
Parent or Guardian:			Address (of parent/guardian):	

To be completed by dentist:

Oral Health Status (check all that apply)

☐ Yes ☐ No **Dental Sealants Present**

☐ Yes ☐ No **Caries Experience / Restoration History** — A filling (temporary/permanent) OR a tooth that is missing because it was extracted as a result of caries OR missing permanent 1st molars.

☐ Yes ☐ No **Untreated Caries** — At least 1/2 mm of tooth structure loss at the enamel surface. Brown to dark-brown coloration of the walls of the lesion. These criteria apply to pit and fissure cavitated lesions as well as those on smooth tooth surfaces. If retained root, assume that the whole tooth was destroyed by caries. Broken or chipped teeth, plus teeth with temporary fillings, are considered sound unless a cavitated lesion is also present.

☐ Yes ☐ No **Soft Tissue Pathology**

☐ Yes ☐ No **Malocclusion**

Treatment Needs (check all that apply)

☐ **Urgent Treatment** — abscess, nerve exposure, advanced disease state, signs or symptoms that include pain, infection, or swelling

☐ **Restorative Care** — amalgams, composites, crowns, etc.

☐ **Preventive Care** — sealants, fluoride treatment, prophylaxis

☐ **Other** — periodontal, orthodontic

Please note _____

Signature of Dentist _____   Date of Exam _____

Address _____   Telephone _____
            Street   City   ZIP Code

Illinois Department of Public Health, Division of Oral Health
217-785-4899 • TTY (hearing impaired use only) 800-547-0466 • www.idph.state.il.us

IOCI 0600-10   Printed by Authority of the State of Illinois

Illinois State Board of Education (6/10)

Immunization, Health, Dental and Vision Requirements Illinois Law in the School Office

Sample Form 6-3: Dental Examination Waiver Form

State of Illinois
Department of Public Health

DENTAL EXAMINATION WAIVER FORM

Please print:

Student's Name:	Last	First	Middle	Birth Date: (Month/Day/Year) / /
Address: Street		City	ZIP Code	Telephone:
Name of School:		Grade Level:		Gender: ☐ Male ☐ Female
Parent or Guardian:		Address (of parent/guardian):		

I am unable to obtain the required dental examination because:

☐ My child is enrolled in the free and reduced lunch program and is not covered by private or public dental insurance (Medicaid/All Kids).

☐ My child is enrolled in the free and reduced lunch program and is ineligible for public insurance (Medicaid/All Kids).

☐ My child is enrolled in Medicaid/All Kids, but we are unable to find a dentist or dental clinic in our community that is able to see my child and will accept Medicaid/All Kids.

☐ My child does not have any type of dental insurance, and there are no low-cost dental clinics in our community that will see my child.

Signature _____ Date _____

Illinois Department of Public Health, Division of Oral Health
217-785-4899 • TTY (hearing impaired use only) 800-547-0466 • www.idph.state.il.us

December 2006

Illinois State Board of Education (12/06)

Illinois Law in the School Office   Immunization, Health, Dental and Vision Requirements

Sample Form 6-4: Eye Examination Report

**State of Illinois
Eye Examination Report**

Illinois law requires that proof of an eye examination by an optometrist or physician (such as an ophthalmologist) who provides eye examinations be submitted to the school no later than October 15 of the year the child is first enrolled or as required by the school for other children. The examination must be completed within one year prior to the first day of the school year the child enters the Illinois school system for the first time. The parent of any child who is unable to obtain an examination must submit a waiver form to the school.

Student Name _____
                            (Last)   (First)   (Middle Initial)
Birth Date _____ Gender _____ Grade _____
           (Month/Day/Year)
Parent or Guardian _____
                            (Last)   (First)
Phone _____
      (Area Code)
Address _____
          (Number)   (Street)   (City)   (ZIP Code)
County _____

To Be Completed By Examining Doctor

Case History
Date of exam _____

Ocular history: ❏ Normal   or Positive for _____

Medical history: ❏ Normal   or Positive for _____

Drug allergies: ❏ NKDA   or Allergic to _____

Other information _____

Examination

	Distance			Near
	Right	Left	Both	Both
Uncorrected visual acuity	20/	20/	20/	20/
Best corrected visual acuity	20/	20/	20/	20/

Was refraction performed with dilation? ❏ Yes ❏ No

	Normal	Abnormal	Not Able to Assess	Comments
External exam (lids, lashes, cornea, etc.)	❏	❏	❏	_____
Internal exam (vitreous, lens, fundus, etc.)	❏	❏	❏	_____
Pupillary reflex (pupils)	❏	❏	❏	_____
Binocular function (stereopsis)	❏	❏	❏	_____
Accommodation and vergence	❏	❏	❏	_____
Color vision	❏	❏	❏	_____
Glaucoma evaluation	❏	❏	❏	_____
Oculomotor assessment	❏	❏	❏	_____
Other _____	❏	❏	❏	_____

NOTE: "Not Able to Assess" refers to the inability of the child to complete the test, not the inability of the doctor to provide the test.

Diagnosis
❏ Normal   ❏ Myopia   ❏ Hyperopia   ❏ Astigmatism   ❏ Strabismus   ❏ Amblyopia

Other _____

Page 1   *Continued on back*

Immunization, Health, Dental and Vision Requirements   Illinois Law in the School Office

State of Illinois
Eye Examination Report

Recommendations

1. Corrective lenses: ❏ No   ❏ Yes, glasses or contacts should be worn for:
   ❏ Constant wear   ❏ Near vision   ❏ Far vision
   ❏ May be removed for physical education

2. Preferential seating recommended: ❏ No   ❏ Yes
   Comments _____
   _____

3. Recommend re-examination: ❏ 3 months   ❏ 6 months   ❏ 12 months
   ❏ Other _____

4. _____

5. _____

Print name _____   License Number _____
Optometrist or physician (such as an ophthalmologist)
who provided the eye examination ❏ MD ❏ OD ❏ DO

| **Consent of Parent or Guardian** |
| I agree to release the above information on my child or ward to appropriate school or health authorities. |

Address _____

_____

(Parent or Guardian's Signature)

Phone _____

(Date)

Signature _____   Date _____

(Source: Amended at 32 Ill. Reg. _____, effective _____)

Page 2

Printed by Authority of the State of Illinois
6/09

IOCI1271-09

Illinois State Board of Education (6/09)

— 102 —

Sample Form 6-5: Eye Examination Waiver Form

**State of Illinois
Department of Public Health
Eye Examination Waiver Form**

Please print:

Student Name _____ Birth Date _____
　　　　　　　　　(Last)　　　　　　　　　(First)　　　　　　(Middle Initial)　　　　(Month/Day/Year)

School Name _____ Grade Level _____ Gender ❏ Male ❏ Female

Address _____
　　　　　(Number)　　　　(Street)　　　　　　　　(City)　　　　　　　(ZIP Code)

Phone _____
　　　(Area Code)

Parent or Guardian _____
　　　　　　　　　(Last)　　　　　　　　　　　　　(First)

Address of Parent or Guardian _____
　　　　　　　　　　　　　　(Number)　　(Street)　　　(City)　　　(ZIP Code)

I am unable to obtain the required vision examination because:

❏ My child is enrolled in medical assistance/ALL KIDS, but we are unable to find a medical doctor who performs eye examinations or an optometrist in the community who is able to examine my child and accepts medical assistance/ALL KIDS.

❏ My child does not have any type of medical or vision/eye care coverage, my child does not qualify for medical assistance/ALL KIDS, there are no low-cost vision/eye clinics in our community that will see my child, and I have exhausted all other means and do not have sufficient income to provide my child with an eye examination.

❏ Other undue burden or a lack of access to an optometrist or to a physician who provides eye examinations: _____
_____

Signature _____ Date _____

(Source: Added at 32 Ill. Reg. _____, effective _____)

Illinois State Board of Education (6/09)

References

105 ILCS 5/27-8.1. Health Examinations and Immunizations.

(1) In compliance with rules and regulations which the Department of Public Health shall promulgate, and except as hereinafter provided, all children in Illinois shall have a health examination as follows: within one year prior to entering kindergarten or the first grade of any public, private, or parochial elementary school; upon entering the sixth and ninth grades of any public, private, or parochial school; prior to entrance into any public, private, or parochial nursery school; and, irrespective of grade, immediately prior to or upon entrance into any public, private, or parochial school or nursery school, each child shall present proof of having been examined in accordance with this Section and the rules and regulations promulgated hereunder. Any child who received a health examination within one year prior to entering the fifth grade for the 2007-2008 school year is not required to receive an additional health examination in order to comply with the provisions of Public Act 95-422 when he or she attends school for the 2008-2009 school year, unless the child is attending school for the first time as provided in this paragraph.

A tuberculosis skin test screening shall be included as a required part of each health examination included under this Section if the child resides in an area designated by the Department of Public Health as having a high incidence of tuberculosis. Additional health examinations of pupils, including eye examinations, may be required when deemed necessary by school authorities. Parents are encouraged to have their children undergo eye examinations at the same points in time required for health examinations.

(1.5) In compliance with rules adopted by the Department of Public Health and except as otherwise provided in this Section, all children in kindergarten and the second and sixth grades of any public, private, or parochial school shall have a dental examination. Each of these children shall present proof of having been examined by a dentist in accordance with this Section and rules adopted under this Section before May 15th of the school year. If a child in the second or sixth grade fails to present proof by May 15th, the school may hold the child's report card until one of the following occurs: (i) the child presents proof of a completed dental examination or (ii) the child presents proof that a dental examination will take place within 60 days after May 15th. The Department of Public Health shall establish, by rule, a waiver for children who show an undue burden or a lack of access to a dentist. Each public, private, and parochial school must give notice of this dental examination requirement to the parents and guardians of students at least 60 days before May 15th of each school year.

(1.10) Except as otherwise provided in this Section, all children enrolling in kindergarten in a public, private, or parochial school on or after the effective date of this amendatory Act of the 95th General Assembly and any student enrolling for the first time in a public, private, or parochial school on or after the effective date of this amendatory Act of the 95th General Assembly shall have an eye examination. Each of these children shall present proof of having been examined by a physician licensed to practice medicine in all of its branches or a licensed optometrist within the previous year, in accordance with this Section and rules adopted under this Section, before October 15th of the school year. If the child fails to present proof by October 15th, the school may hold the child's report card until one of the following occurs: (i) the child presents proof of a completed eye examination or (ii) the child presents proof that an eye examination will take place within 60 days after October 15th. The Department of Public Health shall establish, by rule, a waiver for children who show an undue burden or a lack of access to a physician licensed to practice medicine in all of its branches who provides eye examinations or to a licensed optometrist. Each public, private, and parochial school must give notice of this eye examination requirement to the parents and guardians of students in compliance with rules of the Department of Public Health. Nothing in this Section shall be construed to allow a school to exclude a child from attending because of a parent's or guardian's failure to obtain an eye examination for the child.

(2) The Department of Public Health shall promulgate rules and regulations specifying the examinations and procedures that constitute a health examination, which shall include the collection of data relating to obesity (including at a minimum, date of birth, gender, height, weight, blood pressure, and date of exam), and a dental examination and may recommend by rule that certain additional examinations be performed. The rules and regulations of the Department of Public Health shall specify that a tuberculosis skin test screening shall be included as a required part of each health examination included under this Section if the child resides in an area designated by the Department of Public Health as having a high incidence of tuberculosis. The Department of Public Health shall specify that a diabetes screening as defined by rule shall be included as a required part of each health examination. Diabetes testing is not required.

Physicians licensed to practice medicine in all of its branches, advanced practice nurses who have a written collaborative agreement with a collaborating physician which authorizes them to perform health examinations, or physician assistants who have been delegated the performance of health examinations by their supervising physician shall be responsible for the performance of the health examinations, other than dental examinations, eye examinations, and vision and hearing screening, and shall sign all report forms required by subsection (4) of this Section that pertain to those portions of the health examination for which the physician, advanced practice nurse, or physician assistant is responsible. If a registered nurse performs any part of a health examination, then a physician licensed to practice medicine in all of its branches must review and sign all required report forms. Licensed dentists shall perform all dental examinations and shall sign all report forms required by subsection (4) of this Section that pertain to the dental examinations. Physicians licensed to practice medicine in all its branches or licensed optometrists shall perform all eye examinations required by this Section and shall sign all report forms required by subsection (4) of this Section that pertain to the eye examination. For purposes of this Section, an eye examination shall at a minimum include history, visual acuity, subjective refraction to best visual acuity near and far, internal and external examination, and a glaucoma evaluation, as well as any other tests or observations that in the professional judgment of the doctor are necessary. Vision and hearing screening tests, which shall not be considered examinations as that term is used in this Section, shall be conducted in accordance with rules and regulations of the Department of Public Health, and by individuals whom the Department of Public

Health has certified. In these rules and regulations, the Department of Public Health shall require that individuals conducting vision screening tests give a child's parent or guardian written notification, before the vision screening is conducted, that states, "Vision screening is not a substitute for a complete eye and vision evaluation by an eye doctor. Your child is not required to undergo this vision screening if an optometrist or ophthalmologist has completed and signed a report form indicating that an examination has been administered within the previous 12 months."

(3) Every child shall, at or about the same time as he or she receives a health examination required by subsection (1) of this Section, present to the local school proof of having received such immunizations against preventable communicable diseases as the Department of Public Health shall require by rules and regulations promulgated pursuant to this Section and the Communicable Disease Prevention Act.

(4) The individuals conducting the health examination, dental examination, or eye examination shall record the fact of having conducted the examination, and such additional information as required, including for a health examination data relating to obesity (including at a minimum, date of birth, gender, height, weight, blood pressure, and date of exam), on uniform forms which the Department of Public Health and the State Board of Education shall prescribe for statewide use. The examiner shall summarize on the report form any condition that he or she suspects indicates a need for special services, including for a health examination factors relating to obesity. The individuals confirming the administration of required immunizations shall record as indicated on the form that the immunizations were administered.

(5) If a child does not submit proof of having had either the health examination or the immunization as required, then the child shall be examined or receive the immunization, as the case may be, and present proof by October 15 of the current school year, or by an earlier date of the current school year established by a school district. To establish a date before October 15 of the current school year for the health examination or immunization as required, a school district must give notice of the requirements of this Section 60 days prior to the earlier established date. If for medical reasons one or more of the required immunizations must be given after October 15 of the current school year, or after an earlier established date of the current school year, then the child shall present, by October 15, or by the earlier established date, a schedule for the administration of the immunizations and a statement of the medical reasons causing the delay, both the schedule and the statement being issued by the physician, advanced practice nurse, physician assistant, registered nurse, or local health department that will be responsible for administration of the remaining required immunizations. If a child does not comply by October 15, or by the earlier established date of the current school year, with the requirements of this subsection, then the local school authority shall exclude that child from school until such time as the child presents proof of having had the health examination as required and presents proof of having received those required immunizations which are medically possible to receive immediately. During a child's exclusion from school for noncompliance with this subsection, the child's parents or legal guardian shall be considered in violation of Section 26-1 and subject to any penalty imposed by Section 26-10. This subsection (5) does not apply to dental examinations

and eye examinations. Until June 30, 2015, if the student is an out-of-state transfer student and does not have the proof required under this subsection (5) before October 15 of the current year or whatever date is set by the school district, then he or she may only attend classes (i) if he or she has proof that an appointment for the required vaccinations has been scheduled with a party authorized to submit proof of the required vaccinations. If the proof of vaccination required under this subsection (5) is not submitted within 30 days after the student is permitted to attend classes, then the student is not to be permitted to attend classes until proof of the vaccinations has been properly submitted. No school district or employee of a school district shall be held liable for any injury or illness to another person that results from admitting an out-of-state transfer student to class that has an appointment scheduled pursuant to this subsection (5).

(6) Every school shall report to the State Board of Education by November 15, in the manner which that agency shall require, the number of children who have received the necessary immunizations and the health examination (other than a dental examination or eye examination) as required, indicating, of those who have not received the immunizations and examination as required, the number of children who are exempt from health examination and immunization requirements on religious or medical grounds as provided in subsection (8). Every school shall report to the State Board of Education by June 30, in the manner that the State Board requires, the number of children who have received the required dental examination, indicating, of those who have not received the required dental examination, the number of children who are exempt from the dental examination on religious grounds as provided in subsection (8) of this Section and the number of children who have received a waiver under subsection (1.5) of this Section. Every school shall report to the State Board of Education by June 30, in the manner that the State Board requires, the number of children who have received the required eye examination, indicating, of those who have not received the required eye examination, the number of children who are exempt from the eye examination as provided in subsection (8) of this Section, the number of children who have received a waiver under subsection (1.10) of this Section, and the total number of children in noncompliance with the eye examination requirement. This reported information shall be provided to the Department of Public Health by the State Board of Education.

(7) Upon determining that the number of pupils who are required to be in compliance with subsection (5) of this Section is below 90% of the number of pupils enrolled in the school district, 10% of each State aid payment made pursuant to Section 18-8.05 to the school district for such year may be withheld by the State Board of Education until the number of students in compliance with subsection (5) is the applicable specified percentage or higher.

(8) Parents or legal guardians who object to health, dental, or eye examinations or any part thereof, or to immunizations, on religious grounds shall not be required to submit their children or wards to the examinations or immunizations to which they so object if such parents or legal guardians present to the appropriate local school authority a signed statement of objection, detailing the grounds for the objection. If the physical condition of the child is such that any one or more of the immunizing agents should not be administered, the examining physician, advanced practice nurse, or physician assistant

responsible for the performance of the health examination shall endorse that fact upon the health examination form. Exempting a child from the health, dental, or eye examination does not exempt the child from participation in the program of physical education training provided in Sections 27-5 through 27-7 of this Code.

(9) For the purposes of this Section, "nursery schools" means those nursery schools operated by elementary school systems or secondary level school units or institutions of higher learning.

Additional Reference Materials

(All referenced materials can be found on the Illinois General Assembly website at www.ilga.gov.)

Illinois Laws:

1)   Child Vision and Hearing Test Act [410 ILCS 205]
2)   Medical Practice Act of 1987 [225 ILCS 60]
3)   Illinois Optometric Practice Act of 1987 [225 ILCS 80]
4)   School Breakfast and Lunch Program Act [105 ILCS 125]
5)   Illinois Dental Practice Act [225 ILCS 25]
6)   Nurse Practice Act [225 ILCS 65]
7)   Physician Assistant Practice Act of 1987 [225 ILCS 95]
8)   Lead Poisoning Prevention Act [410 ILCS 45]

Illinois Administrative Rules:

1)   Control of Tuberculosis Code (77 Ill. Adm. Code 696)
2)   Vision Screening (77 Ill. Adm. Code 685)
3)   Hearing Screening (77 Ill. Adm. Code 675)
4)   Control of Communicable Diseases Code (77 Ill. Adm. Code 690)
5)   Immunization Code (77 Ill. Adm. Code 695)

Chapter 7

Special Student Populations

"Talent comes with an individual name tag."
– Charles Handy

In This Chapter:

- 7.1 Introduction
- 7.2 Special Education
- 7.3 Section 504 of the Rehabilitation Act of 1973
- 7.4 Response to Intervention
- 7.5 Low Income Students and Families
- 7.6 Homeless Students
- 7.7 Foster Children
- 7.8 Undocumented Students
- 7.9 Homeschool Students
- 7.10 Students with Special Religious Needs

FAQs
Checklists and Sample Forms
References

7.1 Introduction

Article X of the Illinois Constitution provides that a "fundamental goal…of the State is the development of all persons to the limits of their capacities." As such, a public school district is required to meet the needs of a wide range of student populations. This chapter provides basic information on the rights of special student populations and the corresponding responsibilities of a public school district. For specific information regarding residency and enrollment, see Chapter 2.

7.2 Special Education

Generally:

Both State and Federal law govern the educational needs of children with disabilities. The Federal law, the Individuals with Disabilities Education Act, better known as IDEA, provides the underlying requirements for special education and is reinforced and supplemented by additional State obligations.

Under IDEA and State law, school districts are responsible for ongoing "child find" activities to determine if children age birth through 21 (the day before a child's twenty-second birthday) are eligible for special education and related services. There are numerous categories of special education eligibility, including: mental retardation, deaf-blindness, deafness, emotional disturbance, developmental delay, traumatic brain injury, visual impairment, hearing impairment, orthopedic impairment, intellectual disability, autistic, speech or language impairment, multiple disabilities and other health impairment. If a child's disability is found to impact educational performance, the child qualifies for special education and related services.

The IEP:

An Individualized Education Program or IEP is a personal education plan designed to meet the unique needs of a child with disabilities. It is intended to help a child reach educational goals more easily than he or she otherwise would. An IEP is required by State and Federal law for each child who receives special education services. The IEP is a legally binding document that must be followed in guiding the child's educational needs. The IEP generally contains the child's current educational status, goals and objectives, instructional setting or placement, transitional services and due process requirements.

The IEP is reviewed annually by the child's IEP team in order to measure student progress and make any necessary modifications or adjustments. Reevaluation of the need for special education services takes place at least every three years.

IEP Team:

The IEP team consists of the student's parent, special education teacher(s), regular education teacher(s), a school representative, an individual who can interpret evaluation results, other individuals who have knowledge or special expertise regarding the child and the child, when appropriate. Other individuals may be included upon agreement of the IEP team members. The purpose of the IEP team is to jointly make decisions that are in the best interest of the child.

A child's parent is an equal member of the IEP team and has the right to attend all IEP meetings. A parent may also request an IEP meeting at any time, which the school district must accommodate or provide a satisfactory explanation as to why such meeting is not necessary. Parents who disagree with a school or IEP team can generally challenge decisions through an array of due process procedures.

Graduation and Transitional Services:

A student with a disability who has fulfilled the minimum State graduation requirements must be awarded a regular high school diploma. Once a student receives a high school diploma, special education services terminate. If the student's IEP requires transitional services beyond the graduation date, the student's high school diploma is deferred until all services are completed. Note, however, a student with an IEP must be allowed to participate in the graduation ceremony with his or her grade appropriate classmates regardless of whether or not the student is eligible to receive a diploma at that time.

7.3 Section 504 of the Rehabilitation Act of 1973

Generally:

Section 504 is a part of the Rehabilitation Act of 1973, which prohibits discrimination based on a person's disabilities. Under Section 504, individuals with disabilities are persons with a physical or mental impairment that "substantially limits one or more major life activities," like walking, seeing, hearing, speaking, breathing or learning. Disabilities addressed by Section 504 include both short and long-term conditions, including: cancer, dyslexia, allergies, depression, asthma or a broken leg. If a student has a 504 qualifying disability that impacts the student's access to education, a school district must make reasonable accommodations to place the student on equal footing with his or her non-disabled peers.

The 504 Plan:

Eligible students receive a 504 Plan, which takes into consideration the student's unique needs and provides reasonable accommodations. Examples of accommodations include extra time to get to class or complete an assignment, enlarged print or visual aids, assistance in taking notes and a medication delivery plan.

Section 504 Plans are reduced to writing and should be coordinated with the student, parent and all appropriate school personnel.

Difference from Special Education:

Section 504 is designed to make reasonable accommodations to put students on par with their non-disabled peers. Special education is designed to provide students with services to address their disabling condition(s). As such, all students who are eligible for special education services are 504 eligible, but not all 504 students are eligible for special education services.

Rights of Parents and School District:

As discussed above, parents must consent to special education placement for their child. Section 504 does not require a parent to consent to evaluation or services. A 504 team makes the final decision regarding eligibility and accommodations. A parent must, however, be given a copy of the 504 Plan if the student is found eligible for accommodations.

If a parent disagrees with the district's decision, the district's 504 coordinator can help to resolve differences informally. If informal procedures fail, the parent may request a hearing before an impartial hearing officer.

7.4 Response to Intervention

Response to Intervention or RtI is a new program that is mandatory in Illinois public schools as of January 2009. In a nutshell, RtI is a process of establishing learning environments that are effective for all students.

In the RtI process, teachers, individually and collectively, carefully monitor each student's educational progress. As soon as a student begins to fall behind in a certain subject or subjects, the school provides that student with instructional interventions targeted to the student's particular needs.

RtI is not special education and is geared toward all students. In fact, successful RtI interventions often prevent the need for special educational services by correcting student needs and behaviors as soon as they are identified.

In Illinois, there are three academic and three behavioral tiers to RtI. The following chart provided by the Illinois State Board of Education illustrates these three tiers.

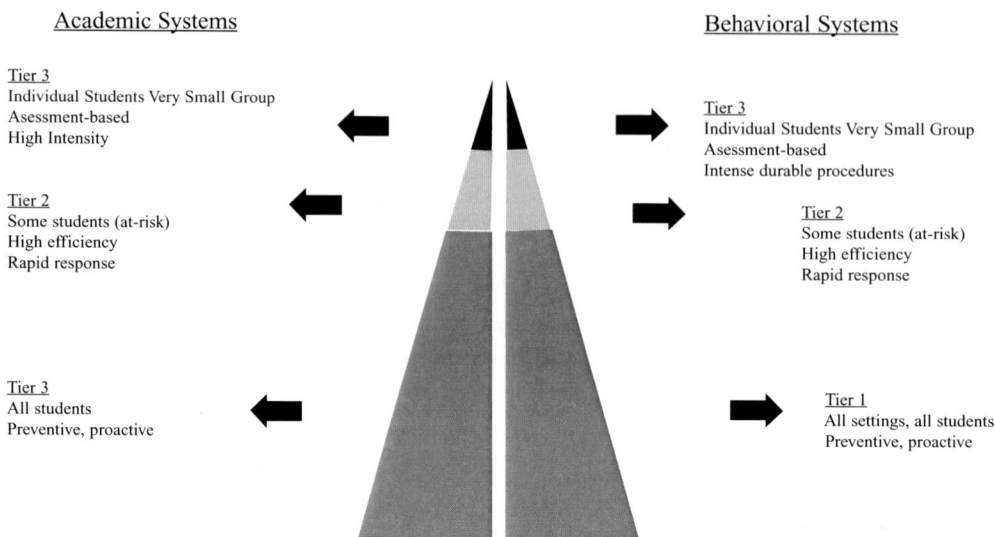

Tier 1 consists of proactive and preventative interventions and generally meets the needs of 80 percent of students. Tier 2 provides more specific targeted intervention (either behavioral or academic), while Tier 3 provides the most intensive interventions, which may include small group and individual work to supplement the core curriculum.

Note that while parents have the right to decline special education, parents do not have the right to refuse RtI interventions.

7.5 Low Income Students and Families

Free and Reduced-Price Meals:

Eligibility for free and reduced-price food services is determined by the income eligibility guidelines, family-size income standards, set annually by the U.S. Department of Agriculture. Students who meet the income eligibility guidelines are eligible for free or reduced priced meals. For 2011-12 eligibility, see Checklist 7-1.

In providing services to students, a school must be careful not to publically identify students receiving free or reduced-price meals. Methods for collecting meal payments must prevent identification of children receiving assistance.

Textbook and Activity Fee Waivers:

Low income students and families may not be denied benefits of a public education based on income. Therefore, fees for textbooks, instructional materials, driver education, athletics and other activities are usually waived for students who meet the eligibility criteria.

Students are eligible for a fee waiver when the student currently lives in a household that meets the same income guidelines, with the same limits based on household size, that are used for the Federal free meals program. A school district may also consider other factors in determining a fee waiver, such as illness in the family, unemployment and emergency situations.

7.6 Homeless Students

Under State and Federal law, a student is homeless if the student lacks a fixed nighttime abode or, put simply, does not have a permanent place to live. A student is also considered homeless if the student's permanent residence is a shelter or other place not intended as a place for people to live. The definition of homeless also includes individuals sharing a residence due to loss of housing or economic hardship or living in a hotel, trailer park or campgrounds due to a lack of alternative adequate accommodations.

There is no specific time limit on how long a child or youth can be considered homeless. Whether a child or youth meets the definition of being homeless depends on their living situation and individual circumstances.

A homeless student may not be denied enrollment in a school district due to his or her failure to produce normally required enrollment documents, such as academic records, medical records and proof of residency. Additionally, homeless students are generally eligible for free meals and a full fee waiver.

School districts are also required to provide or arrange transportation for homeless students. If a homeless student is attending school in a district that is different from where the student is temporarily living, both school districts must agree to a division of transportation costs or split such costs equally if an agreement cannot be reached.

Each school district is required to have a homeless liaison, who should be contacted for additional questions regarding a school's responsibilities and the educational rights of homeless students.

7.7 Foster Children

Foster children who are five or older by September 1 are required by the Department of Children and Family Services to attend school. Foster children generally attend the school where their foster parents reside, although DCFS is ultimately responsible for determining the appropriate school for a foster child. Additionally, by law, foster children are entitled to participate in free breakfast and lunch programs and receive free textbooks. For further information on the education of children in foster care, see Checklist 7-2.

7.8 Undocumented Students

In the case of *Plyler v. Doe*, the United States Supreme Court determined that a child of illegal immigrants cannot be denied a public education. As such, the immigration status of the parent or child has no bearing on the rights of the student to enroll. School districts may not question a child's immigration status as part of the enrollment process. A school district may not, as part of a residency inquiry, require that parents or adult caretakers provide a Visa, "Green Card," Illinois driver's license, a state identification card or other documents that require a Social Security number.

The parent of an undocumented student must still prove residency, provide the child's birth certificate and comply with physical and immunization laws, as well as all other admission requirements.

7.9 Homeschool Students

Overview:

Illinois is recognized as one of the friendliest states in terms of a parent's ability to provide a homeschool education. Because homeschools are not specifically provided for in Illinois law, they are governed the same as private schools, which are virtually unregulated. Once a parent makes the decision to provide a child with a home-based education, the State, regional office and education and local school district must take a hands-off approach. State and local authorities are not allowed to monitor the student's academic progress or mandate that the child take State achievement tests. There is also no requirement that the homeschool teacher possess any type of certification.

The Decision to Homeschool:

Once a parent notifies school officials that the parent will be providing a home school education, the public school must release the student to the parent. It is strongly suggested that parents complete written documentation (see sample Form 7-1) officially notifying school officials and the regional office of education that the student will be educated in a home-based facility; however, such documentation cannot be required of the homeschool parent.

Textbooks, Academic Materials and Access:

Public schools are not required to provide homeschool students textbooks and other academic materials. A public school may, however, loan homeschool students books, tests and other materials that are not needed by the school to educate its full-time student population.

School districts generally have discretion as to whether or not to allow homeschool students to participate on a part-time basis. Technically, homeschool parents must notify the public school district by the first day of May if they wish for their child to attend part-time during the following year; however, this requirement can be waived by the district.

According to State law, a public school that offers driver's education must allow homeschool students to participate. A public school district, by policy, can determine whether or not a homeschool child who lives in the district boundaries is eligible to participate in athletics.

Returning to Full-Time Attendance:

Statistics show that a vast majority of homeschool students either enroll or reenroll in the public school system at some point. This most frequently occurs when a student is high school-aged. A school district has complete discretion to test a homeschool student and place the student in the grade where the student belongs academically, regardless of age. Additionally, a public school has the right to require that a certain number of credits are earned at the school before a child is eligible for a diploma or class honors.

Special Education Services:

Homeschool students may be eligible for special education services. Generally, however, a parent must bring the child to the public school for services. Consult your school administrator for additional information.

7.10 Students with Special Religious Needs

A school district must take great care not to burden a student's freedom of religion. Because religion is perhaps our most sacred constitutional right, students are generally allowed to fully participate in religious dress and customs while at school. This includes wearing of traditional headgear and clothing and being allowed accommodations to pray during the school day, as required by religious tenants.

The Illinois School Code also clearly provides that students must be excused from school (an excused absence) for religious observations and holidays. A school district cannot take any negative actions against a student for school time missed for valid religious reasons.

FAQs

What is the Individuals with Disabilities Education Act?

The Individuals with Disabilities Education Act, better known as IDEA, is a Federal law mandating special education services for children with certain disabilities. IDEA is reinforced and supplemented by additional State obligations. For additional information, see Section 7.2.

What is an Individualized Education Program?

An Individualized Education Program or IEP is a personal education plan designed to meet the unique needs of a child with disabilities. It is intended to help a child reach educational goals more easily than he or she otherwise would. For additional information, see Section 7.2.

What is a 504 Plan?

Section 504 is a part of the Rehabilitation Act of 1973. A 504 plan is designed to eliminate barriers to one's education by providing reasonable accommodations. For additional information, see Section 7.3.

How is Section 504 different from IDEA?

Section 504 is designed to make reasonable accommodations to put students on par with their non-disabled peers. Special education is designed to provide students with services to address their disabling condition(s).

What is Response to Intervention?

Response to Intervention or RtI is a new program that is mandatory in Illinois public schools as of January 2009. In a nutshell, RtI is a process of establishing learning environments that are effective for all students. For more information, see Section 7.4.

Is RtI the same as special education?

RtI is not special education and is geared toward all students. In fact, successful RtI interventions often prevent the need for special education services by correcting student needs and behaviors as soon as they are identified.

What students are eligible for free and reduced-price meals?

Eligibility for free and reduced-price food services is determined by the income eligibility guidelines, family-size income standards, set annually by the U.S. Department of Agriculture. Students who meet the income eligibility guidelines are eligible for free or reduced priced meals. For 2011-12 eligibility, see Checklist 7-1.

Are students who are eligible for free and reduced-price meals also given a fee waiver for school activities?

Low income students and families may not be denied benefits of a public education based on their income. Therefore, fees for textbooks, instructional materials, driver education, athletics and other activities are usually waived for students who meet the eligibility criteria. For additional information, see Section 7.5.

What is the definition of "homeless"?

Under State and Federal law, a student is homeless if the student lacks a fixed nighttime abode or, put simply, does not have a permanent place to live. A student is also considered homeless if the student's permanent residence is a shelter or other place not intended as a place for people to live. The definition of homeless also includes individuals sharing a residence due to loss of housing or economic hardship or living in a hotel, trailer park or campground due to a lack of alternative adequate accommodations.

Should a homeless student be enrolled in school if he or she does not have the proper registration documents?

A homeless student may not be denied enrollment in a school district due to his or her failure to produce normally required enrollment documents, such as academic records, medical records and proof of residency.

Who is responsible for making decisions for foster children?

Decisions regarding foster children fall primarily on the Department of Children and Family Services. Foster parents are allowed to make several decisions for children in their care. For specific information, see Checklist 7-2.

Are undocumented students allowed to enroll in school?

In the case of *Plyler v. Doe*, the United States Supreme Court determined that a child of illegal immigrants cannot be denied a public education. As such, the immigration status of the parent or child has no bearing on the rights of the student to enroll.

What documentation is required before a child can be homeschooled?

Once parents notify school officials that they will be providing a homeschool education, the public school must release the student to the parent. It is strongly suggested that parents complete written documentation (see sample Form 7-1) officially notifying school officials and the regional office of education that the student will be educated in a home-based facility; however, such documentation cannot be required of the homeschool parent.

Can a homeschool student participate on a part-time basis?

School districts generally have discretion as to whether or not to allow homeschool students to participate on a part-time basis. A public school that offers driver's education must allow homeschool students to participate. A public school district, by policy, can determine whether or not a homeschool child who lives in the district boundaries is eligible to participate in athletics. For more information, see Section 7.9.

Must a school district accommodate a student's religious needs while at school?

A school district must take great care not to burden a student's freedom of religion. Because religion is perhaps our most sacred constitutional right, students are generally allowed to fully participate in religious dress and customs while at school. This includes wearing of traditional headgear and clothing and being allowed accommodations to pray during the school day, as required by religious tenants. For more information, see Section 7.10.

Checklists and Sample Forms

Sample forms available at www.edlawyer.org

Checklist 7-1: 2011-12 Income Eligibility Guidelines for Free and Reduced-Price Lunch Eligibility

FISCAL YEAR 2012 INCOME ELIGIBILITY GUIDELINES
The United States Department of Agriculture has issued the following income guidelines for the period July 1, 2011, through June 30, 2012

Free Meals 130% Federal Poverty Guidelines					
Household Size	Annual Month	Monthly Weeks	Twice Per	Every Two	Weekly
1	14,157	1,180	590	545	273
2	19,123	1,594	797	736	368
3	24,089	2,008	1,004	927	464
4	29,055	2,422	1,211	1,118	559
5	34,021	2,836	1,418	1,309	655
6	38,987	3,249	1,625	1,500	750
7	43,953	3,663	1,832	1,691	846
8	48,919	4,077	2,039	1,882	941
For each additional family member add	4,988	414	207	191	98

Reduced-Price Meals 185% Federal Poverty Guidelines					
Household Size	Annual Month	Monthly Weeks	Twice Per	Every Two	Weekly
20,147	1,698	840	775	388	
2	27,214	2,268	1,134	1,047	524
3	34,281	2,857	1,429	1,319	660
4	41,348	3,446	1,723	1,591	796
5	48,415	4,035	2,018	1,863	932
6	55,482	4,624	2,312	2,134	1,067
7	62,549	5,213	2,607	2,406	1,203
8	69,616	5,802	2,901	2,678	1,339
,For each additional family member add	7,067	589	295	272	136

The following is the definition of income:
Income is defined as any monies earned before any deductions such as income taxes, social security taxes, insurance premiums, charitable contributions, and bonds. It includes the following (1) monetary compensation for services including wages, salary, commissions, or fees; (2) net income from non-farm self-employment; (3) net income from farm self-employment; (4) social security; (5) dividends or interest on savings or bonds or income from estates or trusts; (6) net rental income; (7) public assistance or welfare payments; (8) unemployment compensation; (9) government civilian employee or military retirement or pensions or veteran payments; (10) private pensions or annuities; (11) alimony or child support payments; (12) regular contributions from persons not living in the household; (13) net royalties; and (14) other cash income. Other cash income would include cash amounts received or withdrawn from any source including savings, investments, trust accounts, and other resources which would be available to pay the price of a child's meal.

United States Department of Agriculture. For updated information, see:
http://www.fns.usda.gov/cnd/governance/notices/iegs/iegs.htm

Checklist 7-2: Who Has the Responsibility for Students in Foster Care?

(This form indicates who should be contacted when dealing with school issues for students in foster care.)

Duty	Foster Parent	DCFS Worker
Enroll the child in the free breakfast and lunch programs	X	
Attend school conferences and handle routine school matters, including receipt of report card	X	
Contact regarding child's injuries at school	X	
Obtain permission for the child to attend in-state school trips	X	
Obtain permission for the child to attend out-of-state school trips		X
Sign liability releases and most other legal documents		X
Approve the child's participation in extra-curricular school activities, except athletic participation	X	
Approve the child's participation in athletic events		X
Consent to release of medical information and school records and other school information		X
Appeal education plans, suspensions and expulsions		X
Handle most special education issues on behalf of the child	X	

Information adapted from Illinois Department of Children and Family Services, Foster Parent Rights and Responsibilities, 2002

Illinois Law in the School Office Special Student Populations

Sample Form 7-1: Home Schooling Registration

Illinois State Board of Education
Data Analysis and Progress Reporting
100 North First Street, S-284
Springfield, Illinois 62777-0001
Telephone #: 217/782-3950   Fax #: 217/524-7784

Home Schooling Registration
School Year Beginning in Fall _____ (provide year)

Directions: Please complete all areas of this form and return it to the Illinois State Board of Education at the address above. This form is electronically fillable or you may print a copy and complete it by hand—**PLEASE PRINT**.

PLEASE REMEMBER TO REGISTER EVERY SEPTEMBER.
Registration with the Illinois State Board of Education and/or your Regional Office of Education is voluntary.

NAME(S) OF PARENT(S) OR GUARDIAN(S)		COUNTY	
ADDRESS (Street, City, State, Zip Code)	TELEPHONE (Include Area Code)	FAX (Include Area Code)	
	E-MAIL		

Provide the full name of each child being taught and information for the current school year:

NAME	GRADE	GENDER		DATE OF BIRTH (mm/dd/yyyy)
		MALE	FEMALE	
		☐	☐	___/___/___
		☐	☐	___/___/___
		☐	☐	___/___/___
		☐	☐	___/___/___
		☐	☐	___/___/___

Provide information on the last public or nonpublic school attended (if applicable):

CHILD	SCHOOL NAME	PUBLIC/NONPUBLIC (Check only one)		DATES OF ATTENDANCE (mm/dd/yyyy)
		☐	☐	___/___/___
		☐	☐	___/___/___
		☐	☐	___/___/___
		☐	☐	___/___/___
		☐	☐	___/___/___

Provide the name of the curriculum to be used: _____

Education areas being taught (•heck all that apply):
(Section 26-1 of the School Code states that areas of education must be taught in the English language)

☐ Language Arts   ☐ Mathematics   ☐ Biological and Physical Sciences

☐ Social Sciences   ☐ Fine Arts   ☐ Physical Development and Health

Other (please specify) _____

_____   _____
Signature of Parent/Guardian   Date (mm/dd/yyyy)

ISBE 87-02 (6/10)

Illinois State Board of Education Form 87-02 (6/10)

References

105 ILCS 10-20.24. Part-time attendance.

To accept in part-time attendance in the regular education program of the district pupils enrolled in nonpublic schools if there is sufficient space in the public school desired to be attended. Request for attendance in the following school year must be submitted by the nonpublic school principal to the public school before May 1. Request may be made only to those public schools located in the district where the child attending the nonpublic school resides.

To accept, pursuant to the provisions of Section 14-6.01, in part-time attendance resident pupils of the types described in Sections 14-1.02 through 14-1.07 who are enrolled in nonpublic schools.

Additional Reference Materials

(All referenced Illinois materials can be found on the Illinois General Assembly website at www.ilga.gov. Links to the Federal materials are provided below.)

Illinois Laws:

1) Children with Disabilities [105 ILCS 5/14-1.01, *et seq.*]
2) Education for Homeless Children Act [105 ILCS 45/1-1, *et seq.*]

Federal Laws:

1) Individuals with Disabilities Education Act [20 USC 1400, *et seq.*]
   http://idea.ed.gov
2) Section 504 of the Rehabilitation Act of 1973 [29 USC 794]
   http://www.dol.gov/oasam/regs/statutes/sec504.htm
3) McKinney-Vento Homeless Assistance Act of 2001 [42 U.S.C. 11431 *et seq.*]
   http://www2.ed.gov/programs/homeless/legislation.html

Chapter 8

Handling Money and School Account Management

"Honesty is the best policy - when there is money in it."
– Mark Twain

In This Chapter:

      8.1   Introduction
      8.2   Basic Money Management
      8.3   Handling Cash from Events and Fundraisers
      8.4   Student Activity Accounts
      8.5   Petty Cash Accounts
      8.6   Revolving Fund Accounts
      8.7   Credit Cards and Procurement Cards

Checklists
FAQs
References

8.1 Introduction

One of the most daunting tasks for school support staff is handling and accounting for money that routinely passes through the school building. This can include a check brought in by a parent or reconciling funds from the previous night's basketball game.

Over the past several years, there have been a number of high profile cases where school employees were accused of stealing money from their district. We have no doubt that a vast majority of these cases amount to nothing more than sloppy bookkeeping and entry errors. However, if money cannot be properly accounted for, fingers will be pointed and the accusation will be theft! And in an attempt to prove your innocence, lost money is very difficult to track and account for.

Because school support staff members are routinely placed in the position of handling money, the purpose of this chapter is twofold. First, we will discuss State laws and administrative rules governing money management at the school level. Second, we will offer tips and advice for effectively handling and managing money.

8.2 Basic Money Management

First and foremost, it is critical to follow your school district and school accounting practices and procedures. Each school district is required to have a policy delineating who can handle money and the specific safeguards that must be utilized. It is recommended that school support staff members who are expected to handle money discuss with their supervisor: (1) district and school policies and procedures that are in place; and (2) the employee's specific responsibilities in handling money.

All money (cash and checks) that comes into the school should be overseen by at least three employees to assure accurate recordkeeping and to protect each person handling the funds. For example:

- Employee 1 (generally a receptionist or secretary) should open mail and collect money. This employee should make a tape of all receipts and endorse all checks as "for deposit only."
- Employee 2 (generally a school secretary or bookkeeper) should properly record all money and prepare the funds for deposit by separately listing all amounts on a deposit slip. This individual can also make the actual deposit at the bank.
- Employee 3 (the account custodian / supervisor who is generally the principal) should make sure that the list of receipts, the deposit slip and the deposit receipt are consistent.

Also, anyone serving as the official treasurer of a school account should be bonded. Bonding is a process where a bonding company assures that a person is qualified to serve as treasurer of the fund. If the fund is not properly maintained and there is a loss of money, the bonding company generally covers the loss.

8.3 Handling Cash from Events and Fundraisers

Handling cash from events and fundraisers brings about special concerns, especially when the funds are transported from location to location. The following are generally acceptable accounting techniques that assure accuracy and protect money handlers.

1. All activities requiring the collection of money must be approved by the school principal or other authorized agent of the school district. If an organization seeks to have a fundraiser, the appropriate application must be completed and approved before the activity begins.
2. Teachers, coaches, class sponsors, etc. should never keep money in their possession over night.
3. At the end of each day, money should be counted and brought to the school office or other designated location. The appropriate office personnel should count the money again and issue a receipt.
4. From here, school policy and procedures should be followed for depositing the money into the proper bank account.

8.4 Student Activity Accounts

The school board may establish certain activity funds to be managed by student organizations. Student activity funds are defined as funds owned, operated and managed by organizations, clubs or associations within the student body under the guidance and direction of one or more staff members for educational, recreational or cultural purposes. Examples of student activity funds include: homeroom, yearbook, class year, choral or band group, class projects, student clubs, student council and student-sponsored bookstore. It is critical that student activity accounts are only used for activities that support students. Use of these funds for non-student activities is illegal.

The advantage of a student activity account is that the account can be managed by the treasurer without the school board taking action to expend funds from the account. However, it is important to note that student activity funds must be maintained under the guidance and direction of a staff member in the district. Student activity accounts must also be reconciled monthly. A report that includes a statement of receipts must be provided to activity group members and the school board on a monthly basis.

If the school board subsidizes a portion of the activity fund, that portion must be reported as an expenditure or disbursement against the board's regular budget and as a revenue or cash receipt by the activity fund.

If the relevant activity is discontinued, or there has been no activity for one year, the money in a student activity account must be transferred to another activity fund, to the district's funds or to members of the activity group on a pro rata basis.

8.5 Petty Cash Accounts

Petty cash fund means money that is set aside for the purpose of making change or making immediate payments when the amounts involved are so small that processing through the school board's regular procedure would be uneconomical.

Petty cash is perhaps the account that is most prone to mismanagement because money is quickly and routinely taken from this account to pay a variety of day-to-day expenses. In order to assure accurate accounting, State law requires the following in terms of petty cash management:

1. Deposits into a petty cash fund are to be made by authorized check drawn payable to the designated account custodian, who is generally the principal.
2. Each disbursement of money from the account must be approved by the signature of a person other than the account custodian, who is generally the support staff person "in charge" of the account.
3. Petty cash vouchers must be pre-numbered. Each voucher must be accounted for as being used, voided or unused.
4. The person paying the cash out of the petty cash account must sign the voucher.
5. The account custodian must attach to each petty cash voucher the receipt for the disbursement and note the proper expenditure account code.
6. When the petty cash is depleted, the account custodian takes the petty cash vouchers to the appropriate person who then issues a check so that the fund can be replenished.

8.6 Revolving Fund Accounts

A revolving fund account is similar to a petty cash account, except that it is maintained at a bank. In order to draw a check from this account, a person must have proper documentation approved by the school or district, such as a voucher, signed travel reimbursement form, purchase requisition or invoice. Upon presentation of the proper documentation, the bank issues a check.

8.7 Credit Cards and Procurement Cards

Schools and districts also use credit cards and procurement cards. Procurements cards are generally preferred, as these cards allow a school district to specify qualified users, control the amount of expenditures and limit the authorized vendors who can accept the card for purchases. If you are authorized to use the school district's credit card or procurement card, you should: (1) make sure to provide receipts and other required documentation; (2) never use the card for personal items or expenses (even if you plan to reimburse the school district); and (3) maintain a list of usage, just in case there is ever a discrepancy on the account.

FAQs

Should I be bonded if I handle money?
Anyone serving as the official treasurer of a school account should be bonded. For additional information, see Section 8.2.

Is it okay to be the only person who counts and deposits money coming into the school?
No! All money (cash and checks) that comes into the school should be overseen by at least three employees to assure accurate recordkeeping and to protect each person handling the funds. For additional information, see Section 8.2.

What is a student activity account?
Student activity funds are defined as funds owned, operated and managed by organizations, clubs or associations within the student body under the guidance and direction of one or more staff members for educational, recreational or cultural purposes. For additional information, see Section 8.4.

What is petty cash?
Petty cash fund means cash that is set aside for the purpose of making change or making immediate payments when the amounts involved are so small that processing through the school board's regular procedure would be uneconomical. For additional information, see Section 8.5

What is a revolving fund?
A revolving fund account is similar to a petty cash account, except that it is maintained at a bank. For more information, see Section 8.6

What is a procurement card?
A procurement card is like a credit card, but the school district has more control to specify qualified users, control the amount of expenditures and limit the authorized vendors who can accept the card for purchases. For more information, see Section 8.7.

Checklists

Checklist 8-1: Money Handling Don'ts

When Handling Cash and Checks, <u>NEVER:</u>

- **Cash a personal check out of a school district account**
- **Take home money at the end of an event**
- **Maintain a negative account balance**
- **Sign checks in advance**
- **Make a personal loan from a school district account**
- **Give away free tickets. Tickets equal a cash sale!**
- **Pay an employee or worker out of ticket revenues**
- **Turn in money without getting a receipt**
- **Be solely responsible for counting and depositing money**

References

> **TITLE 23: EDUCATION AND CULTURAL RESOURCES**
> **SUBTITLE A: EDUCATION**
> **CHAPTER I: STATE BOARD OF EDUCATION**
> **SUBCHAPTER c: FINANCE**
> **PART 100 REQUIREMENTS FOR ACCOUNTING, BUDGETING, FINANCIAL REPORTING, AND AUDITING**
> **SECTION 100.80 STUDENT ACTIVITY FUNDS**

Section 100.80 Student Activity Funds

The requirements of this Section shall apply to student activity funds established by a school board pursuant to Section 10-20.19(3) of the School Code [105 ILCS 5/10-20.19(3)]

a) The board shall take the following actions with respect to each fund:
   1) approve the fund's establishment and purpose;
   2) set policies for students' participation and for supervision by adults;
   3) approve the collection of all monies;
   4) cause records to be kept that will verify the amounts received and disbursed and the assets on hand;
   5) appoint a treasurer, bonded in accordance with Section 8-2 of the School Code [105 ILCS 5/8-2], who will be the custodian of the fund's assets and perform the duties listed in subsection (c) of this Section;
   6) determine whether the treasurer will be authorized to invest any of the fund's assets;
   7) designate depositories for cash and any investments;
   8) determine the method of distribution of earnings from investments, if any;
   9) determine whether, and under what circumstances, loans may be transacted between funds;
   10) if the relevant activity has been discontinued, or if there has been no activity for one year, transfer money to another activity fund, to the district's funds, or to members of the activity group on a pro rata basis; and
   11) designate the individuals who will have authority to approve written purchase orders or other authorizations that will be required in order to spend funds in instances in which the provisions of Section 10-20.21 of the School Code do not apply and those who will have authority to conduct procurement activities when those provisions do apply.

b) Each activity group shall deposit any funds received from any source with the activity fund's treasurer and obtain a signed receipt identifying the activity fund and the amount.

c) The treasurer of each activity fund shall:
   1) be the fund's sole custodian;

2) keep all monies in a depository designated in accordance with Section 8-7 of the School Code [105 ILCS 5/8-7] or invest them in conformance with the Public Funds Investment Act [30 ILCS 235] and maintain liability accounts to show the ownership of all assets;

3) make all disbursements from the fund by a treasurer's check drawn upon the fund;

4) write checks only when sufficient funds are on hand to cover them;

5) reconcile the bank and investment balances with the fund's liabilities monthly;

6) provide to group members and the school board a monthly report that includes a statement of receipts, disbursements, and current balances;

7) carry the fund's balance over to the next fiscal year unless otherwise instructed by the school board; and

8) make loans between activity funds, if and as authorized by the board's policy.

d) If the board subsidizes a portion of an activity fund, that portion shall be reported as an expenditure or disbursement against the board's regular budget and as a revenue or cash receipt by the activity fund.

TITLE 23: EDUCATION AND CULTURAL RESOURCES
SUBTITLE A: EDUCATION
CHAPTER I: STATE BOARD OF EDUCATION
SUBCHAPTER c: FINANCE
PART 100 REQUIREMENTS FOR ACCOUNTING, BUDGETING, FINANCIAL REPORTING, AND AUDITING
SECTION 100.70 REVOLVING FUNDS

Section 100.70 Revolving Funds

The requirements of this Section shall apply to revolving funds and petty cash funds established by a school board pursuant to Section 10-20.19(2) of the School Code [105 ILCS 5/10-20.19(2)].

a) Each resolution shall establish the school board's policy as to the amounts and types of payments that shall be made from the fund, state the amount at which the fund shall be established, designate a custodian of the fund, and require that the fund be maintained in compliance with Section 10-20.19 of the School Code and all other applicable statutes.

b) In the case of a petty cash fund:
   1) The resolution shall also authorize a check in the amount of the fund to be drawn payable to the designated custodian.
   2) Each disbursement shall be approved by the signature of a person other than the custodian.
   3) Each petty cash voucher shall be pre-numbered and each shall be accounted for as having been used, voided, or unused. Each petty cash voucher shall also provide for the signature of the person to whom cash is paid.
   4) The custodian shall attach to each petty cash voucher the receipt for the disbursement made and shall note the proper expenditure account code or provide sufficient descriptive information to allow assignment of the correct code.
   5) When the larger part of the cash on hand has been disbursed, the custodian shall take the paid petty cash vouchers to the person authorized to prepare and issue checks so that the fund can be replenished.

c) In the case of any revolving fund other than a petty cash fund:
   1) The resolution shall also provide that the fund shall be maintained in a bank.
   2) The total of all checks written since the last reimbursement plus the bank balance for the checking account shall equal the amount set aside for the revolving fund.
   3) No check shall be issued without presentation of pre-approved documentation for the expenditure, such as a signed voucher, a completed and approved travel request, an approved purchase requisition, an order, or an invoice. The record for each check written shall include the expense account code or sufficient descriptive information to allow assignment of the correct code.
   4) At regular intervals, the revolving fund shall be reimbursed up to its original amount. The check written for this reimbursement shall be included on the school

board's monthly listing of bills, charging the appropriate expenditure accounts and indicating the recipient and explanation for each revolving fund check that was issued.

d) If a school board has obtained and issued credit cards or procurement cards for the use of board members, the superintendent, or other district employees or officials to pay certain job-related expenses or to make purchases on behalf of the board or district or any student activity funds, or for purposes that would otherwise be addressed through a conventional revolving fund, then the board shall adopt a written credit card policy that at least:

1) identifies the allowable types of purchases;
2) provides for the issuing bank to block the cards' use at unapproved merchants;
3) limits the amount a card-holder can charge in a single purchase or within a given month;
4) provides specific guidelines on purchases via telephone, fax, and the Internet;
5) indicates the consequences for unauthorized purchases;
6) requires card-holders to sign a statement affirming that they are familiar with the board's credit card policy;
7) requires review and approval of purchases by someone other than the card-holder or user;
8) requires submission of original receipts to document purchases;
9) forbids the use of a card to make purchases in a manner contrary to the requirements of Section 10-20.21 of the School Code [105 ILCS 5/10-20.21]; and
10) indicates how financial or material rewards or rebates are to be accounted for and treated.

Chapter 9

Transportation and Related Issues

"Everyone is in awe of the lion tamer in a cage with half a dozen lions-everyone but a school bus driver."
– Dr. Laurence J. Peter

In This Chapter:

9.1 Introduction
9.2 Types of Allowable Transportation
9.3 Pupil Transportation Reimbursement
9.4 Transportation of Homeless Students
9.5 Transportation of Students with Disabilities
9.6 School Bus Communication Devices
9.7 Bus Pre-Trip and Post-Trip Inspection
9.8 Post Bus Accident Procedures

Checklists
FAQs
References

9.1 Introduction

One of the most important responsibilities of a school district is the safe and efficient transportation of students to and from school and school-related activities. Most school districts (including community consolidated districts, community unit districts, consolidated districts and consolidated high school districts), are required to provide free transportation for pupils residing at least one and one-half miles from the school they are required to attend.

This chapter discusses the various legal aspects of providing transportation to students, including reimbursement for transportation costs.

9.2 Types of Allowable Transportation

In 2010, there were major changes to student transportation laws. These new laws strictly govern the types of vehicles that may be used to transport students to and from school and school events.

When a school or district is transporting students to and from a "curriculum-related school activity" (defined as home to school, between attendance centers, to vocational or career centers, to a regional safe school or any other program where academic credit is given), only the following transportation vehicles can be used:

1. A school bus;
2. A municipal bus (with certain restrictions); or

3. A vehicle manufactured to transport not more than ten persons, including the driver. (Examples of these vehicles include a car, station wagon, mini-van, taxi cab, medic-van, and suburban.)

If a school or school district is transporting students to and from interscholastic or athletic activities that are not part of required instruction, the following transportation vehicles may be used:

1. A school bus;
2. A vehicle manufactured to transport not more than ten persons, including the driver; or
3. A multifunction school-activity bus (MFSAB).

Effective July 1, 2010, cargo vans designed to carry between 11 and 15 persons cannot be used for any type of curricular or extracurricular transportation of school age children.

9.3 Pupil Transportation Reimbursement

Any school district that meets certain qualifications is eligible for partial reimbursement of transportation costs from the State. Claims must be transmitted electronically directly to the Illinois State Board of Education by midnight, August 15 of each year.

Transportation at the beginning and end of the school day and to and from school is generally reimbursable. Transportation that is provided prior to or following voluntary, extracurricular and/or co-curricular activities, including sports practices, club meetings, drama rehearsals or choral and band practices, where such activities are scheduled immediately before or immediately after the school day, qualifies as transportation provided at the beginning or end of the school day and is therefore subject to reimbursement with respect to students who are required to be transported.

Field trips are reimbursable if the following conditions are met:

- The field trip occurs during a day of student attendance included on the official school calendar of the district;
- The field trip occurs during the hours that are part of the claimable clock hours on the General State Aid Claim, i.e., the destination of the trip is considered to be the assigned attendance center for all students enrolled in the class;
- The field trip is provided free of charge to the pupil; and
- The field trip is part of the school's curriculum for which pupil's can earn credit for graduation.

For additional information on the reimbursement claim process, visit the Illinois State Board of Education's website at www.isbe.net. See sample Checklist 9-1 for types of vehicles for which mileage is reimbursable by the State.

9.4 Transportation of Homeless Students

Students who are homeless may generally attend school on a tuition free basis in one of three places:

1. The school in which he or she was enrolled when permanently housed (also known as the "school of origin");

2. The school in which he or she was last enrolled; or
3. Any public school that non-homeless students who live in the attendance area are eligible to attend.

School districts are also required to provide or arrange transportation for homeless students. If a homeless student is attending school in a district that is different from where the student is temporarily living, both school districts must agree to a division of transportation costs or split such costs equally if an agreement cannot be reached.

9.5 Transportation of Students with Disabilities

All students with disabilities who are ages 3-21 and who require transportation as a necessary related service pursuant to their Individualized Education Program (IEP) must be provided transportation. See Checklist 9-2, below for specific requirements regarding transportation of children with disabilities.

9.6 School Bus Communication Devices

Each school bus is required to have either a cellular radio telecommunication device or two-way radio while the school bus driver is in possession of the school bus. The device must be turned on and adjusted in a manner that would alert the driver of an incoming communication request.

State law prohibits a school bus driver from operating a school bus while using a cell phone. Bus drivers may still have cell phones, although they are prohibited from using cell phones for anything, including personal use, while operating a bus except: (1) in an emergency situation to communicate with an emergency response operator, a hospital, a physician's office or health clinic, an ambulance service, a fire department, fire district or fire company or a police department; (2) in the event of a mechanical breakdown or other mechanical problem; (3) to communicate with school authorities or their designees about bus operation or the welfare and safety of any passengers on the bus; or (4) when the bus is parked.

9.7 Bus Pre-Trip and Post-Trip Inspection

School bus drivers, whether employed by the school district or private sector school bus company, are required to perform the following inspection tasks.

Pre-Trip Inspection:

Test the cellular radio communication device or two-way radio and ensure that it is functioning properly before the bus is operated.

Post-Trip Inspection:

Perform a visual sweep for children or other passengers at the end of a route, work shift or workday by:

1. Activating interior lights of the school bus to assist the driver in searching in and under each seat, and
2. Walking to the rear of the school bus/vehicle checking in and under each seat.

If a mechanical post-trip inspection reminder system is installed, the driver must comply with the requirements of that system.

9.8 Post Bus Accident Procedures

In the case of a school bus accident, there are specific protocols and procedures that must be followed. It is primarily important to contact the police and follow any policies or procedures specifically mandated by the school district. These policies should be reviewed in advance and a copy should be kept in each bus for easy reference.

In addition to district requirements, laws often require post-alcohol and drug testing to assure that the bus driver was not under the influence of prohibited substances while in control of the bus. An inspection of the bus must also be done before it can be returned to service. Lastly, a school bus accident report must be completed. See sample Form 9-2 for a bus accident report form approved by the Illinois State Board of Education.

FAQs

Is there a time limit a student can spend on the school bus?
No. However, the Illinois State Board of Education encourages school districts to limit travel time to not more than one hour to school and not more than one hour from school.

If a child is required to serve a detention either before or after school, does the school district have to provide transportation?
Yes. Whenever a school district (that is otherwise required to provide transportation) requires a student to serve a detention either before or after school, the district must provide for or arrange transportation, unless the student lives within one and one-half miles of school. When a detention is scheduled for Saturday or other day when school is not in session, the district is not obligated to provide transportation services.

Are districts required to provide door-to-door transportation for pre-Kindergarten and elementary age students?
No, unless it is required by the Individualized Education Program (IEP) of a student with disabilities.

Is the driver of a school bus required to see that a child reaches his or her home?
No. The responsibility of the driver ends once the child leaves the school bus at the appropriate location.

Is the district required to transport students who live less than one and one-half miles from their school?
No, however, a school district may provide transportation for pupils living less than one and one-half miles from school.

Which school district is responsible for transporting a homeless student if the homeless student is temporarily living outside the school district?
School districts are required to provide or arrange transportation for homeless students. If a homeless student is attending school in a district that is different from where the student is temporarily living, both school districts must agree to a division of transportation costs or split such costs equally if an agreement cannot be reached.

What are the transportation requirements for students with disabilities?
All students with disabilities who are ages 3-21 who require transportation as a necessary related service pursuant to their Individualized Educational Program (IEP) must be provided transportation. See Checklist 9-2, below.

What are the requirements of a school bus driver to unload children safely on a public roadway?
A school bus traveling on a one-way roadway or a highway having four or more lanes must stop for the loading or unloading of students only on the right side of the highway. If the

highway has four or more lanes and permits traffic to operate in both directions, the bus must load or discharge only those students whose residences are located to the right of the highway.

Can a district install recording devices on school buses?
Yes. State law allows both a visual and audio recordings to be made on the interior of a school bus when transportation is provided for any school related activity.

Can a school bus enter private property to drop off or pick up a student?
No. A school bus cannot enter private property without the written consent of the owner of the property.

Are students allowed to eat or drink on a school bus?
This matter is governed solely by district policy. However, the Illinois State Board of Education recommends that students not be allowed to eat or drink on a school bus.

Are children required to wear seat belts on a school bus?
No.

What should be done if a school bus is in an accident?
In the case of a school bus accident, there are specific protocols and procedures that must be followed. It is primarily important to contact the police and follow any policies or procedures specifically mandated by the school district. These policies should be reviewed in advance and a copy should be kept in each bus for easy reference. In addition to district requirements, laws often require post-alcohol and drug testing to assure that the bus driver was not under the influence of prohibited substances while in control of the bus. An inspection of the bus must also be done before it can be returned to service. Lastly, a school bus accident report must be completed.

Checklists and Sample Forms

Sample forms available at www.edlawyer.org

Checklist 9-1: School Vehicle-Type Reimbursement Chart

The Multifunction School Activity Bus (MFSAB) can NOT be used for curriculum related trips.

Vehicle	Vehicle Abbr./Man. Label	Vehicle Description (example)	Passengers	Uses	Driver Requirements	Reimbursable miles
Multifunction School Activity Bus	MFSAB	White school bus	11-15	Non-curriculum only	Valid driver's license	No
Multifunction School Activity Bus	MFSAB	White school bus	15+	Non-curriculum only	CDL license with passenger endorsement	No
School Bus		Yellow school bus		Curriculum related & non-curriculum trips	School bus driver permit	Yes, if curriculum related
Car	Passenger Vehicle	Taxi cab, district-owned car		Curriculum related trips	School bus driver permit (restricted)	Yes, if curriculum related
Car	Passenger Vehicle	Taxi cab, district-owned car		Non-curriculum trips	Valid driver's license	No
Van	MPPV MPV	Passenger vehicle or multi-passenger vehicle	10 or less includes driver	Curriculum related trips	School bus driver permit (restricted)	Yes
Van	MPPV MPV	Passenger vehicle or multi-passenger vehicle	10 or less includes driver	Non-curriculum trips	Valid driver's license	No
Passenger Cargo Vans	Bus, other than scchool bus		11-15	NOT ALLOWED	NOT ALLOWED	NOT ALLOWED

Curriculum related trips include to and from school, from one school to another, or for a curriculum related event or field trip. If attendance at the event is a requirement for a class, the trip is curriculum related.

School districts can claim depreciation for the White Activity Bus or Multifunction School-activity bus (MFSAB, manufactured for the purpose of transporting 11 or more passengers [625 ILCS 5/1-148.3a-5]) starting July 1, 2012. Districts can depreciate the entire cost of the bus over a five year period (20% per year) on the Pupil Transportation Claim Reimbursement System (PTCRS).

Restricted school bus driver permit does not have CDL.

Illinois State Board of Education, updated 09/11

Checklist 9-2. Transportation Requirements for Students with Disabilities

All students with disabilities ages 3-21 with an Individualized Education Program (IEP) who require transportation as a necessary related service shall be provided as the child's disability or the program location may require.

1. Arrival and departure times shall ensure a full instructional day which is comparable to that of the regular education students. Any deviation from this standard must be based upon the individual needs of the child and reflected in the child's IEP.
2. Every effort should be made to limit the child's total travel time to not more than one hour each way to and from the special education facility.
3. The special transportation shall be scheduled in such a way that the child's health and ability to relate to the educational experience are not adversely affected.
4. Vehicles utilized for special transportation shall be adapted to the specific needs of the children receiving this service.
5. Personnel responsible for special transportation shall be given training experiences which will enable them to understand and appropriately relate to children with disabilities.
6. When a district has placed students in a State-operated or nonpublic day program, the district shall provide transportation for the children in that program.
7. When a child is placed in a residential facility, the school district shall provide transportation services for the child's initial trip to the facility and return home at the close of the school term. The district shall likewise provide transportation for the child at the beginning and end of each school term thereafter.
    A. If the district assumes responsibility for transportation arrangements, it shall provide reasonable notice to parents of departure dates and times. It shall in all instances notify the parents within 48 hours after completing those arrangements.
    B. The modes of travel and degree of support and supervision to be provided shall be included in the student's IEP.
    C. The district shall provide transportation services for one round trip home, at a midterm break or at another time as mutually agreed by the district and the parents, and at any additional time when the facility is to be temporarily closed.
    D. The school district shall provide round-trip transportation at any time the district seeks additional diagnostic assessments of the student or if the parent wishes the child to be present during a due process hearing.
    E. The school district shall provide round-trip transportation in emergencies such as serious illness of the child or death or imminent death of an individual in the child's immediate family. "Immediate family" includes a parent, a grandparent, a sibling, or any person who resides in the child's immediate household. If the district questions the severity of an illness of the child or an immediate family member, it may require the opinion of a licensed physician to corroborate the severity of the illness.
    F. The school district may also provide transportation services to encourage family contacts and/or to reintegrate the child into the home and community. The district shall have the authority to determine, upon consultation with the parents, when transportation is appropriate for this purpose and shall incorporate this decision, with the specific reasons for it, into the student's IEP.

From Illinois State Board of Education, Pupil Transportation
Frequently Asked Questions, www.isbe.net

Illinois Law in the School Office

Transportation and Related Issues

Sample Form 9-1: Parent/Guardian State Pupil Transportation Reimbursement

Illinois State Board of Education Form 54-13 (3/99)

Transportation and Related Issues   Illinois Law in the School Office

Sample Form 9-2: Uniform School Bus Accident Report

Use your "Mouse" or "Tab" key to move through the fields. You must use the mouse to mark check boxes. After completing last field, click print button.

ILLINOIS STATE BOARD OF EDUCATION
Funding and Disbursement Division
100 North First Street, E-320
Springfield, Illinois 62777-0001

UNIFORM SCHOOL BUS ACCIDENT REPORT

School District		Bus Owner	
Bus Body Make	Bus Chassis Make	Model Year	V.I.N (Vehicle Identification Number)
Bus Driver Name (Last, First, Middle Init.)	Driver License Number	Citation Issued	Police Report Number (If known)
Location (County)	Date of Accident	Day of Accident	Time of Accident

PART I - SCHOOL BUS PHYSICALLY INVOLVED

1. Type of Accident (Enter only one response):
   - [ ] Between Motor Vehicles
   - [ ] Pedestrian
   - [ ] Other collision (animal, animal-drawn vehicle, streetcar)
   - [ ] Fixed Object (complete question 2)
   - [ ] Pedalcycle
   - [ ] Non collision
   - [ ] Railroad train

2. Complete if Fixed Object Accident (enter only one response, that which caused most damage):
   - [ ] Bridge rail
   - [ ] Fence
   - [ ] Sign
   - [ ] Culvert or head wall
   - [ ] Fire hydrant
   - [ ] Tree
   - [ ] Curb or wall
   - [ ] Guardrail
   - [ ] Utility pole
   - [ ] Embankment
   - [ ] Median barrier
   - [ ] Other, specify _____

3. Did accident result in (enter only one response):
   - [ ] Fatality
   - [ ] Nonincapacitating injury (moderate)
   - [ ] Incapacitating injury (serious)
   - [ ] Possible injury (minor)

3a. Property damage only. If property damage occurred, was it:
   - [ ] More than $500.00
   - [ ] Less than $500

4. Number injured? (See Part III) _____

5. Manner of collision between vehicles or objects:
   - [ ] Angle
   - [ ] Rear-end
   - [ ] Head-on
   - [ ] Other: _____

6. Bus direction analysis (enter only one response):

Collision with Pedestrian		Collision with Other Vehicle	
Intersection	Nonintersection	Intersection	Nonintersection
[ ] Bus going straight	[ ] Bus going straight	[ ] Entering at angle, both moving	[ ] Same direction, both moving
[ ] Bus turning right	[ ] Bus turning right	[ ] Entering same direction both moving	[ ] Opposite direction, both moving
[ ] Bus turning left	[ ] Bus turning left	[ ] Entering opposite direction, both moving	[ ] One vehicle stopped
[ ] Bus backing	[ ] Bus backing	[ ] Other action, specify	[ ] Other action, specify
[ ] Other action, specify	[ ] Other action, specify		
All Other Collisions		**Noncollision**	
Intersection	Nonintersection	Intersection	Nonintersection
[ ] Fixed object	[ ] Fixed object	[ ] Overturn	[ ] Overturn
[ ] Other road vehicle, training, pedalcycle	[ ] Other road vehicle, train, pedalcycle	[ ] Other noncollision	[ ] Other noncollision
[ ] Other object, animal	[ ] Other object, animal		

7. First point of impact (enter only one response): _____

ISBE 50-26 (10/07)

8. Contributing circumstances (mark with an "x" as many responses as applicable):

Driver Action	Bus Driver Action	Other Vehicle Driver Action	Roadway
Speed	☐	☐	☐ Defective surface
Right of way-failed to yield	☐	☐	☐ Slippery
Passed stop sign	☐	☐	☐ Inoperative traffic signal
Disregarded signal	☐	☐	☐ View obstructed by object (e.g., tree, fence, shrubbery, etc.)
Drove left of center	☐	☐	**Vehicle Defect**
Improper overtaking	☐	☐	☐ Tires
Made improper turn	☐	☐	☐ Brakes
Followed too closely	☐	☐	☐ Lights
Backing	☐	☐	☐ Steering
Sudden movement	☐	☐	☐ No vehicle defect
No improper action	☐	☐	☐ Other action, specify

9. Total number of lanes on roadway: _____

10. Posted speed limit: _____

11. Approximate speed of the bus: _____

12. Age of school bus driver: _____

13. Driver: ☐ Male ☐ Female

14. Driver's experience driving school bus: ☐ Less than 6 months ☐ 1-2 years ☐ 5-10 years ☐ 1 year or less ☐ 2-5 years ☐ Over 10 years

15. In the last three years how many school bus accidents has the driver had? _____

16. Did the driver receive a pre-service school bus driver training course? ☐ Yes ☐ No

17. Did the driver receive in-service training course in the last 12 months? ☐ Yes ☐ No

18. Was the bus driver's lap belt in use when the accident occurred? ☐ Yes ☐ No

19. Type of school bus: ☐ Type A ☐ Type C ☐ Other ☐ Type B ☐ Type D

20. Total number of passengers on bus (excluding driver): _____

21. Bus rated seating capacity: _____

22. School bus use at time of accident:
☐ Regular route
☐ Field/Activity trip (school related use)
☐ Special Education use
☐ Other use

23. Condition of road at time of accident (enter as many responses as applicable):
☐ Dry ☐ Snow packed
☐ Holes or ruts ☐ Under repair
☐ Icy ☐ West
☐ Muddy ☐ Other, specify _____

24. Light condition (enter only one response):
☐ Dawn
☐ Daylight
☐ Dusk
☐ Dark, artificially illuminated
☐ Dark, not artificially illuminated

25. Weather condition (enter only one response):
☐ Clear ☐ Sleeting
☐ Dust ☐ Smog/smoke
☐ Fog ☐ Snowing
☐ Raining ☐ Other, specify _____

PART II – LOADING/UNLOADING ZONE ACCIDENTS

1. At the time of the accident, where was the bus? (Enter only one response)
☐ Approaching the zone ☐ Stopped in the zone ☐ Leaving the zone ☐ Not in sight

2. Was the pupil(s): ☐ Hit by the bus ☐ Hit by other vehicle

3. Number injured (see part III): _____

4. Location of injured pupil(s):
☐ On side of road ☐ In roadway ☐ On sidewalk ☐ Other, specify _____

ISBE 50-26 (10/07)

Part II - LOADING/UNLOADING ZONE ACCIDENTS (con't.)

Description of accident: (Please describe behavior of pupil(s) in loading zone in this section.)

Complete the following diagram showing direction and positions of vehicles involved, designating clearly the point of contact. (If this diagram will not serve for the accident in question, use adjacent space provided.)

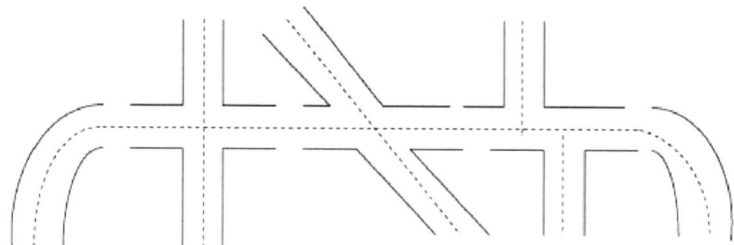

ISBE 50-26 (10/07)

PART III – INJURY TALLY SHEET - SCHOOL TRANSPORTATION-RELATED PERSONNEL

AGE	ON BOARD BUS					OFF BUS LOADING/UNLOADING ZONE				
	KILLED		INJURED			KILLED		INJURED		
			Serious	Moderate	Minor			Serious	Moderate	Minor
	Male	Female	All	All	All	Male	Female	All	All	All
Under 5										
5										
6										
7										
8										
9										
10										
11										
12										
13										
14										
15										
16										
17										
18										
Over 18										
Driver										
Others										
TOTALS										

Report submitted by _____

Signature	Name (Please print):
Date:	Position/Title:

ISBE 50-26 (10/07)

Illinois State Board of Education Form 50-26 (10/07)

References

625 ILCS 5/11-1414.1. School transportation of students.

(a) Every student enrolled in grade 12 or below in any entity listed in subsection (a) of Section 1-182 of this Code must be transported in a school bus or a vehicle described in subdivision (1) or (2) of subsection (b) of Section 1-182 of this Code for any curriculum-related school activity. "Curriculum-related school activity" as used in this subsection (a) includes transportation from home to school or from school to home, tripper or shuttle service between school attendance centers, transportation to a vocational or career center or other trade-skill development site or a regional safe school or other school-sponsored alternative learning program, or a trip that is directly related to the regular curriculum of a student for which he or she earns credit.

(b) Every student enrolled in grade 12 or below in any entity listed in subsection (a) of Section 1-182 of this Code who is transported in a vehicle that is being operated by or for a public or private primary or secondary school, including any primary or secondary school operated by a religious institution, for an interscholastic, interscholastic-athletic, or school-sponsored, noncurriculum-related activity that (i) does not require student participation as part of the educational services of the entity and (ii) is not associated with the students' regular class-for-credit schedule shall transport students only in a school bus or vehicle described in subsection (b) of Section 1-182 of this Code. This subsection (b) does not apply to any second division vehicle used by an entity listed in subsection (a) of Section 1-182 of this Code for a parade, homecoming, or a similar noncurriculum-related school activity.

625 ILCS 5/12-816. Pre and post-trip inspection policy for school buses.

(a) In order to provide for the welfare and safety of children who are transported on school buses throughout the State of Illinois, each school district shall have in place, by January 1, 2008, a policy to ensure that the school bus driver is the last person leaving the bus and that no passenger is left behind or remains on the vehicle at the end of a route, a work shift, or the work day. This policy and procedure shall, at a minimum, require the school bus driver (i) to test the cellular radio telecommunication device or two-way radio and ensure that it is functioning properly before the bus is operated and (ii) before leaving the bus at the end of each route, work shift, or work day, to walk to the rear of the bus and check the bus for children or other passengers in the bus.

(b) If a school district has a contract with a private sector school bus company for the transportation of the district's students, the school district shall require in the contract with the private sector company that the company have a post-trip inspection policy in place. This policy and procedure shall, at a minimum, require the school bus driver (i) to test the cellular radio telecommunication device or two-way radio and ensure that it is functioning properly before the bus is operated and (ii) before leaving the bus at the end of each route, work shift, or work day, to walk to the rear of the bus and check the bus for children or other passengers in the bus.

(c) Before this inspection, the school bus driver shall activate the interior lights of the bus to assist the driver in seeing in and under the seats during a visual sweep of the bus.

(d) This policy may include, at the discretion of the school district, the installation of a mechanical or electronic post-trip inspection reminder system which requires the school bus driver to walk to the rear of the bus to deactivate the system before the driver leaves the bus. The system shall require that when the driver turns off the vehicle's ignition system, the vehicle's interior lights must illuminate to assist the driver in seeing in and under the seats during a visual sweep of the bus.

105 ILCS 5/29-5. Reimbursement by State for transportation.
Reimbursement by State for transportation. Any school district, maintaining a school, transporting resident pupils to another school district's vocational program, offered through a joint agreement approved by the State Board of Education, as provided in Section 10-22.22 or transporting its resident pupils to a school which meets the standards for recognition as established by the State Board of Education which provides transportation meeting the standards of safety, comfort, convenience, efficiency and operation prescribed by the State Board of Education for resident pupils in kindergarten or any of grades 1 through 12 who: (a) reside at least 1 1/2 miles as measured by the customary route of travel, from the school attended; or (b) reside in areas where conditions are such that walking constitutes a hazard to the safety of the child when determined under Section 29-3; and (c) are transported to the school attended from pick-up points at the beginning of the school day and back again at the close of the school day or transported to and from their assigned attendance centers during the school day, shall be reimbursed by the State as hereinafter provided in this Section.

The State will pay the cost of transporting eligible pupils less the assessed valuation in a dual school district maintaining secondary grades 9 to 12 inclusive times a qualifying rate of .05%; in elementary school districts maintaining grades K to 8 times a qualifying rate of .06%; and in unit districts maintaining grades K to 12, including optional elementary unit districts and combined high school--unit districts, times a qualifying rate of .07%; provided that for optional elementary unit districts and combined high school--unit districts, assessed valuation for high school purposes, as defined in Article 11E of this Code, must be used. To be eligible to receive reimbursement in excess of 4/5 of the cost to transport eligible pupils, a school district shall have a Transportation Fund tax rate of at least .12%. If a school district does not have a .12% Transportation Fund tax rate, the amount of its claim in excess of 4/5 of the cost of transporting pupils shall be reduced by the sum arrived at by subtracting the Transportation Fund tax rate from .12% and multiplying that amount by the districts equalized or assessed valuation, provided, that in no case shall said reduction result in reimbursement of less than 4/5 of the cost to transport eligible pupils.

The minimum amount to be received by a district is $16 times the number of eligible pupils transported.

When calculating the reimbursement for transportation costs, the State Board of Education may not deduct the number of pupils enrolled in early education programs from the number of pupils eligible for reimbursement if the pupils enrolled in the early education programs are transported at the same time as other eligible pupils.

Any such district transporting resident pupils during the school day to an area vocational school or another school district's vocational program more than 1 1/2 miles from the school attended, as provided in Sections 10-22.20a and 10-22.22, shall be reimbursed by the State for 4/5 of the cost of transporting eligible pupils.

School day means that period of time which the pupil is required to be in attendance for instructional purposes.

If a pupil is at a location within the school district other than his residence for child care purposes at the time for transportation to school, that location may be considered for purposes of determining the 1 1/2 miles from the school attended.

Claims for reimbursement that include children who attend any school other than a public school shall show the number of such children transported.

Claims for reimbursement under this Section shall not be paid for the transportation of pupils for whom transportation costs are claimed for payment under other Sections of this Act.

The allowable direct cost of transporting pupils for regular, vocational, and special education pupil transportation shall be limited to the sum of the cost of physical examinations required for employment as a school bus driver; the salaries of full or part-time drivers and school bus maintenance personnel; employee benefits excluding Illinois municipal retirement payments, social security payments, unemployment insurance payments and workers' compensation insurance premiums; expenditures to independent carriers who operate school buses; payments to other school districts for pupil transportation services; pre-approved contractual expenditures for computerized bus scheduling; the cost of gasoline, oil, tires, and other supplies necessary for the operation of school buses; the cost of converting buses' gasoline engines to more fuel efficient engines or to engines which use alternative energy sources; the cost of travel to meetings and workshops conducted by the regional superintendent or the State Superintendent of Education pursuant to the standards established by the Secretary of State under Section 6-106 of the Illinois Vehicle Code to improve the driving skills of school bus drivers; the cost of maintenance of school buses including parts and materials used; expenditures for leasing transportation vehicles, except interest and service charges; the cost of insurance and licenses for transportation vehicles; expenditures for the rental of transportation equipment; plus a depreciation allowance of 20% for 5 years for school buses and vehicles approved for transporting pupils to and from school and a depreciation allowance of 10% for 10 years for other transportation equipment so used. Each school year, if a school district has made expenditures to the Regional Transportation Authority or any of its service boards, a mass transit district, or an urban transportation district under an intergovernmental agreement with the district to provide for the transportation of pupils and if the public transit carrier received direct payment for services or passes from a school district within its service area during the 2000-2001 school year, then the allowable direct cost of transporting pupils for regular, vocational, and special education pupil transportation shall also include the expenditures that the district has made to the public transit carrier. In addition to the above allowable costs school districts shall also claim all transportation supervisory salary costs, including Illinois municipal retirement payments, and all transportation related building and building maintenance costs without limitation.

Special education allowable costs shall also include expenditures for the salaries of attendants or aides for that portion of the time they assist special education pupils while in transit and expenditures for parents and public carriers for transporting special education pupils when pre-approved by the State Superintendent of Education.

Indirect costs shall be included in the reimbursement claim for districts which own and operate their own school buses. Such indirect costs shall include administrative costs, or any costs attributable to transporting pupils from their attendance centers to another school building for instructional purposes. No school district which owns and operates its own school buses may claim reimbursement for indirect costs which exceed 5% of the total allowable direct costs for pupil transportation.

The State Board of Education shall prescribe uniform regulations for determining the above standards and shall prescribe forms of cost accounting and standards of determining reasonable depreciation. Such depreciation shall include the cost of equipping school buses with the safety features required by law or by the rules, regulations and standards promulgated by the State Board of Education, and the Department of Transportation for the safety and construction of school buses provided, however, any equipment cost reimbursed by the Department of Transportation for equipping school buses with such safety equipment shall be deducted from the allowable cost in the computation of reimbursement under this Section in the same percentage as the cost of the equipment is depreciated.

On or before August 15, annually, the chief school administrator for the district shall certify to the State Superintendent of Education the district's claim for reimbursement for the school year ending on June 30 next preceding. The State Superintendent of Education shall check and approve the claims and prepare the vouchers showing the amounts due for district reimbursement claims. Each fiscal year, the State Superintendent of Education shall prepare and transmit the first 3 vouchers to the Comptroller on the 30th day of September, December and March, respectively, and the final voucher, no later than June 20.

If the amount appropriated for transportation reimbursement is insufficient to fund total claims for any fiscal year, the State Board of Education shall reduce each school district's allowable costs and flat grant amount proportionately to make total adjusted claims equal the total amount appropriated.

For purposes of calculating claims for reimbursement under this Section for any school year beginning July 1, 1998, or thereafter, the equalized assessed valuation for a school district used to compute reimbursement shall be computed in the same manner as it is computed under paragraph (2) of subsection (G) of Section 18-8.05.

All reimbursements received from the State shall be deposited into the district's transportation fund or into the fund from which the allowable expenditures were made.

Notwithstanding any other provision of law, any school district receiving a payment under this Section or under Section 14-7.02, 14-7.02b, or 14-13.01 of this Code may classify all or a portion of the funds that it receives in a particular fiscal year or from general State aid pursuant to Section 18-8.05 of this Code as funds received in connection with any funding program for which it is entitled to receive funds from the State in that fiscal year (including, without limitation, any funding program referenced in this Section), regardless of the source or timing of the receipt. The district may not classify more funds as funds received in connection with the funding program than the district is entitled to receive in that fiscal year for that program. Any classification by a district must be made by a resolution of its board of education. The resolution must identify the amount of any payments or general State aid to be classified under this paragraph and must specify the funding program to which the funds are to be treated as received in connection therewith. This resolution is controlling as to the classification of funds referenced therein. A certified copy of the resolution must be sent to the State Superintendent of Education. The resolution shall still take effect even though a copy of the resolution has not been sent to the State Superintendent of Education in a timely manner. No classification under this paragraph by a district shall affect the total amount or timing of money the district is entitled to receive under this Code. No classification under this paragraph by a district shall in any way relieve the district from or affect any requirements that otherwise would apply with respect to that funding program, including any accounting of funds by source, reporting expenditures by original source and purpose, reporting requirements, or requirements of providing services.

Any school district with a population of not more than 500,000 must deposit all funds received under this Article into the transportation fund and use those funds for the provision of transportation services.

Chapter 10

Employment Issues and Rights of Non-Certified Staff

"If you love your work, if you enjoy it, you're already a success."
– Jack Canfield, The Success Principles

> **In This Chapter:**
>
> 10.1 Introduction
> 10.2 Personnel Records
> 10.3 Evaluation
> 10.4 Discipline and Dismissal
> 10.5 Overtime Compensation
> 10.6 Religious Holidays
> 10.7 Freedom from Workplace Harassment
> 10.8 Nursing Mothers in the Workplace
> 10.9 Americans with Disabilities Act
> 10.10 Family and Medical Leave Act
> 10.11 Whistleblower Protection
> 10.12 Employee Credit Privacy Act
> 10.13 Equal Pay Act
> 10.14 School Visitation Act
> 10.15 Prohibited Political Activities
> 10.16 Gift Ban Act
> 10.17 Conflicts of Interest
> 10.18 Use of School District Email Accounts
> 10.19 Outside Employment
>
> FAQs
> References

10.1 Introduction

The purpose of this chapter is to make the reader aware of several employment and workplace rights. A full discussion of these rights is beyond the scope of this chapter, though we have tried to highlight those rights most commonly used and asked about. For further information consult the reference materials at the end of this chapter.

Please note, that employees who are in a collective bargaining unit may have rights in addition to those described herein. If you are represented by a union, we strongly recommend consulting your union on all employment issues.

10.2 Personnel Records

Personnel records are primarily governed by the Illinois Personnel Records Review Act, the full text of which can be found in the references materials at the end of this chapter. This law, in a nutshell, provides employees with certain rights with respect to accessing and copying their employment personnel files.

An employment file generally contains information about an employee's qualifications for employment, promotion, transfer, additional compensation, discharge or other disciplinary action. Matters not directly related to employment cannot be maintained in an employee's personnel file.

Upon request, which the employer may require in writing, an employee must be permitted to review and copy his or her personnel file. Generally, access must be provided within seven working days of a request. (An employer can have an additional seven working days to provide access in certain cases.) Unless provided otherwise in a collective bargaining agreement, an employee may generally review his or her personnel record two times each calendar year.

An employee does not, however, have unfettered access to his or her personnel file. Employees are generally not allowed to view letters of reference, test documents, staffing plans, records subject to a pending claim, investigatory and security records and information of a personal nature about another person that would constitute a clear invasion of privacy. All other material in a personnel file must generally be made available to an employee.

An employee who is involved in a current grievance against an employer may designate in writing a representative from the employee's union or collective bargaining unit to inspect the portion of the employee's personnel record that may have a bearing on the resolution of the grievance.

If an employee disagrees with any information contained in the personnel record, the employee and employer may agree to remove or correct the information. If an agreement cannot be reached between the employee and employer, the employee has a right to submit a written statement explaining the employee's position. The employer must attach this statement to the disputed part of the employee's personnel record.

It is also interesting to note, that an employer may not divulge a disciplinary report, letter of reprimand or other disciplinary action to a third party without first providing written notice to the employee, unless the employee has waived the right to such notice. Additionally, employers must generally delete or remove disciplinary reports, letters of reprimand or other records of disciplinary action that are more than four years old.

10.3 Evaluation

Evaluations of non-certified staff are generally governed by board policy. Most policies provide for a summative evaluation each year. If you are in a union, your evaluation tool may be subject to negotiation by your authorized bargaining unit.

Employee evaluations must be placed in an employee's personnel file. As such, employees must be allowed to review any and all evaluations. If there is anything in the evaluation that an employee disagrees with, the employee can submit a rebuttal or explanation, which the employer must attach to the evaluation and place in the employee's personnel file.

10.4 Discipline and Dismissal

Employee discipline and dismissal are generally detailed in the school district's policy manual. If you are in a union, you may have additional rights relative to discipline and dismissal. In addition to the rights provided in policy and the bargaining agreement, a union employee has the right to have a union representative present during an investigative interview. An investigative interview is one where the employee is to be questioned on matters that the employee reasonably believes may lead to discipline or other adverse consequences.

10.5 Overtime Compensation

Most school districts have a policy providing that support staff employees may not work more than 40 hours per week without written permission from their supervisor. In cases were permission is granted, support staff employees must be compensated at 1.5 times their hourly rate of pay for each hour worked over the 40 hour work week. If the school district and employee agree in writing (or the school district and the applicable bargaining unit agree in writing), the school district may provide an employee with 1.5 hours of compensatory time for each hour worked over the 40 hour work week. In most cases, an employee cannot accumulate over 240 hours of compensatory time (representing 160 hours of overtime work).

Note that a school district does not have to pay overtime or provide compensatory time for work on weekends and holidays, as long as an employee's actual work does not exceed 40 hours in the given week.

10.6 Religious Holidays

A school district is not allowed to burden an employee's freedom of religion. An employer is required to allow an employee uncompensated time off from work for all aspects of the employee's religious observations and practices, provided that it does not cause the school district an undue burden. A school district is allowed to require an employee to provide reasonable notice before granting time off for religious reasons.

10.7 Freedom from Workplace Harassment

A school district is required to provide a workplace environment free of harassment based on race, religion, national origin, sex, sexual orientation, age, citizenship status, disability or other protected status. Additionally, unwelcome sexual advances, requests for sexual favors and other verbal or physical conduct or communications constituting harassment on the basis of sex is illegal.

If you feel that you have been harassed based on any of the above factors, you should contact the school district's nondiscrimination coordinator immediately.

10.8 Nursing Mothers in the Workplace

State and Federal law require employers to provide reasonable unpaid break time for an employee to express breast milk for her nursing child. The law also requires an employer to provide a place, other than a bathroom, that is shielded from view and free from intrusion from coworkers and the public that may be used by an employee to express breast milk.

10.9 Americans with Disabilities Act

The Americans with Disabilities Act, better known as the ADA, is a Federal law that prohibits discrimination against persons with disabilities in the workplace. An individual is considered to have a "disability" if he or she has a physical or mental impairment that substantially limits one or more major life activities, has a record of such impairment or is regarded as having such impairment.

The ADA mandates that employers provide reasonable accommodations to employees with disabilities. A reasonable accommodation is any modification or adjustment to a job or the work environment that will enable an employee to perform essential job functions. Reasonable accommodation also requires employers to make adjustments and modifications to assure that employees with disabilities have the exact same rights and privileges as their non-disabled counterparts. Note, an employer does not have to retain an employee with a disability if the employee is unable to perform essential job functions with the required accommodations. Employers are also not required to make accommodations that cause an undue hardship, based on expense, feasibility and other factors. An employer is not required to reallocate essential functions of a job as a reasonable accommodation.

10.10 Family and Medical Leave Act

An employee may be eligible for unpaid family and medical leave (FMLA leave), guaranteed by the Federal Family and Medical Leave Act. Generally, leave can be granted up to a total of 12 weeks each year. Reasons for FMLA leave include:

- The birth and first-year care of a son or daughter
- The adoption or foster placement of a son or daughter
- The serious health condition of an employee's spouse, child or parent
- The employee's own serious health condition
- Certain military deployments of an employee's spouse, child or parent
- To care for the employee's spouse, child, parent or next of kin who is a covered service member with a serious injury or illness

In many cases, an employee may utilize earned sick leave, vacation leave and compensatory time during an FLMA leave.

10.11 Whistleblower Protection

Illinois' Whistleblower Act shields individuals who expose wrongdoing, fraud, corruption or waste within their school district. The Act also provides that an employer may not retaliate against an employee for refusing to participate in an activity that would result in a violation of a State or Federal law.

In particular, the Act provides that a school district is prohibited from retaliating against an employee who blows the whistle through a reprimand, discharge, suspension, demotion or denial of promotion or transfer. Suspected violations of this Act should be immediately reported to the school district's compliance officer. If retaliation occurs, remedies include reinstatement, two times back pay, interest on back pay and payment of reasonable costs and attorneys' fees.

10.12 Employee Credit Privacy Act

An employer is generally prohibited from inquiring about an employee's credit history, obtaining an employee's credit report from a credit reporting agency or discharging or discriminating against an individual due to his or her credit history or credit report.

10.13 Equal Pay Act

The Equal Pay Act prohibits employers from paying unequal wages to men and women for doing the same or substantially similar work, requiring equal skill, effort and responsibility, under similar working conditions for the same employer in the same county, except if the wage difference is based upon a seniority system, a merit system, a system measuring earnings by quantity or quality of production or factors other than gender.

10.14 School Visitation Act

Parents are allowed by State law up to eight hours each school year to attend their child's school conferences or classroom activities, when such activities cannot be scheduled during non-work hours. Leave is limited to four hours per day. School visitation leave is unpaid, but an employer is required to make a good-faith effort to allow an employee to make up the missed time.

10.15 Prohibited Political Activities

Employees are prohibited from intentionally performing any political activities during work time. Furthermore, a school employee cannot, as a condition of employment, be required to perform any political activity during his or her time off, such as holidays, vacation or personal time. An employee may, however, volunteer to do political work during his or her personal time away from work.

Note also that a school district is prohibited from disciplining or discriminating against an employee due to political beliefs.

10.16 Gift Ban Act

School employees are prohibited from accepting gifts from a "prohibited source." A prohibited source generally includes any individual or business that does business with the school district. The gift ban also applies to an employee's spouse and immediate family members.

There are several exemptions to the gift ban, some of which include:

- Opportunities, benefits and services that are available on the same conditions to the general public
- Anything for which an employee pays the fair market value
- Educational materials
- Travel expenses for a meeting to discuss business
- A gift from a relative
- Anything provided by an individual on the basis of a personal friendship, unless such gift is intended to garner influence
- Food or refreshments not exceeding $75 per person in value on a single calendar day
- Any item or items from any one prohibited source during any calendar year having a cumulative total value of less than $100

Employees are allowed to accept gifts from their employers, including school board members, without fear of violating the Gift Ban Act.

10.17 Conflicts of Interest

No school employee is allowed to have a financial interest (directly or indirectly) in any contract, work or business of the school district or in the sale of any article to the district.

10.18 Use of School District Email Accounts

Almost all school staff members have electronic mail or e-mail addresses that are routed through the school or district's technology network. Furthermore, many staff members are able to access their e-mail accounts from home computers or another computer that is off of school property. Additionally, staff members generally have the ability to access their personal email accounts through the school district's server.

School employees should take great care to follow the district's acceptable use policy, which outlines the appropriate uses of the school district's email accounts and the school district's server. In addition to these policies and procedures, we believe two points are critical:

1. Your school district issued email account should only be used for official school business. School officials, and in many cases the public at large, have the right to review emails sent or received on your school district issued account.

2. You should never access your personal email account through the school district's server. Again, school officials may be able to access your personal emails sent through the district's technology network.

10.19 Outside Employment

A school district cannot prohibit an employee from "moonlighting" or having another job outside the school district, except in cases where an employee's second job interferes with his or her assigned school district duties.

FAQs

Am I allowed to review my personnel record?

Yes. Employees are generally allowed to review their personnel record on two occasions during each calendar year. For more information, see Section 10.2.

Can my employer charge a fee for copying my personnel record?

An employer may charge a fee to copy your personnel record; however, the fee must be limited to the actual cost of duplicating the information.

What can be done if I disagree with a portion of my personnel record?

If an employee disagrees with any information contained in the personnel record, the employee and employer may agree to remove or correct the information. If an agreement cannot be reached between the employee and employer, the employee has a right to submit a written statement explaining the employee's position. The employer must attach this statement to the disputed part of the employee's personnel record.

How long may my employer maintain copies of disciplinary documents?

Employers must generally delete or remove disciplinary reports, letters of reprimand or other records of a disciplinary action that are more than four years old. For more information, see Section 10.2.

Can I see a copy of my evaluation?

Yes. Your employer must allow you to review your evaluation. You are also entitled to a copy of your evaluation upon request.

What rights do I have if I am disciplined by my employer?

Employee discipline and dismissal are generally detailed in the school district's policy manual. If you are in a union, you may have additional rights relative to discipline and dismissal. In addition to the rights provided in policy and the bargaining agreement, a union employee has the right to have a union representative present during an investigative interview. An investigative interview is one where the employee is to be questioned on matters that the employee reasonably believes may lead to discipline or other adverse consequences.

Am I entitled to overtime compensation for extra hours worked?

Yes. Support staff employees must be compensated at 1.5 times their hourly rate of pay for each hour worked over the 40 hour work week. If the school district and employee agree in writing (or the school district and the applicable bargaining unit agree in writing), the school district may provide an employee with 1.5 hours of compensatory time for each hour worked over the 40 hour work week. For more information, see Section 10.5.

Can a school district deny my request for time off for religious reasons?

No. An employer is required to allow an employee uncompensated time off from work for all aspects of the employee's religious observations and practices, provided that it does not cause the school district an undue burden. For more information, see Section 10.6.

What rights do nursing mothers have in the workplace?
State and Federal law require employers to provide reasonable unpaid break time for an employee to express breast milk for her nursing child. The law also requires an employer to provide a place, other than a bathroom, that is shielded from view and free from intrusion from coworkers and the public that may be used by an employee to express breast milk.

What is the Americans with Disabilities Act?
The Americans with Disabilities Act, better known as the ADA, is a Federal law that prohibits discrimination against persons with disabilities in the workplace. An individual is considered to have a "disability" if he or she has a physical or mental impairment that substantially limits one or more major life activities, has a record of such impairment, or is regarded as having such impairment. For more information, see Section 10.9.

Can I take extended unpaid leave if I get sick or to care for a sick family member?
Yes. Under the Family and Medical Leave Act (FMLA), employees are generally granted up to a total of 12 weeks each year for illness or to care for ill family members. In many cases, an employee may use earned sick leave, vacation leave and compensatory time during an FLMA leave. For more information, see Section 10.10.

Am I protected if I report corruption in my school district?
Yes, Illinois' Whistleblower Act shields individuals who expose wrongdoing, fraud, corruption or waste within their school district. The Act also provides that an employer may not retaliate against an employee for refusing to participate in an activity that would result in a violation of a State or Federal law. For more information, see Section 10.11.

Can my employer ask about my credit or credit history?
An employer is generally prohibited from inquiring about an employee's credit history, obtaining an employee's credit report from a credit reporting agency or discharging or discriminating against an individual due to his or her credit history or credit report.

Can I be paid a lower salary based on my gender?
No. The Equal Pay Act prohibits employers from paying unequal wages to men and women for doing the same or substantially similar work, requiring equal skill, effort and responsibility, under similar working conditions for the same employer in the same county, except if the wage difference is based upon a seniority system, a merit system, a system measuring earnings by quantity or quality of production or factors other than gender.

Can I take time off to participate in my child's education?
Parents are allowed by State law up to eight hours each school year to attend their child's school conferences or classroom activities, when the activities cannot be scheduled during non-work hours. Leave is limited to four hours per day. School visitation leave is unpaid, but an employer is required to make a good-faith effort to allow an employee to make up the missed time.

Can I be required to donate my time to a school district political issue?
No. A school employee cannot, as a condition of employment, be required to perform any political activity during his or her time off, such as holidays, vacation or personal time. For more information, see Section 10.15.

Can I volunteer to do school district political work on school time?
No. Political work can never be done when you are working. For more information, see Section 10.15.

Can I be fired because of my political beliefs?
No. A school district is prohibited from disciplining or discriminating against an employee due to political beliefs.

Can I accept a gift from someone who does business with the school district?
There are strict limitations on accepting a gift from an individual or company that does business with a school district. These limitations not only apply to an employee, but the employee's family as well. For more information, see Section 10.16.

Can I "moonlight" or hold a second job outside the school district?
Yes, as long as the employment does not interfere with your ability to fulfill your assigned school duties. For more information, see Section 10.19.

References

820 ILCS 5/40-0.01, et seq. Personnel Record Review Act.

§ 0.01. Short title. This Act may be cited as the Personnel Record Review Act.

§ 1. Definitions. As used in this Act:

(a) "Employee" means a person currently employed or subject to recall after layoff or leave of absence with a right to return at a position with an employer or a former employee who has terminated service within the preceding year.

(b) "Employer" means an individual, corporation, partnership, labor organization, unincorporated association, the State, an agency or a political subdivision of the State, or any other legal, business, or commercial entity which has 5 employees or more than 5 employees exclusive of the employer's parent, spouse or child or other members of his immediate family and includes an agent of the employer.

§ 2. Open Records. Every employer shall, upon an employee's request which the employer may require be in writing on a form supplied by the employer, permit the employee to inspect any personnel documents which are, have been or are intended to be used in determining that employee's qualifications for employment, promotion, transfer, additional compensation, discharge or other disciplinary action, except as provided in Section 10. The inspection right encompasses personnel documents in the possession of a person, corporation, partnership, or other association having a contractual agreement with the employer to keep or supply a personnel record. An employee may request all or any part of his or her records, except as provided in Section 10. The employer shall grant at least 2 inspection requests by an employee in a calendar year when requests are made at reasonable intervals, unless otherwise provided in a collective bargaining agreement. The employer shall provide the employee with the inspection opportunity within 7 working days after the employee makes the request or if the employer can reasonably show that such deadline cannot be met, the employer shall have an additional 7 days to comply. The inspection shall take place at a location reasonably near the employee's place of employment and during normal working hours. The employer may allow the inspection to take place at a time other than working hours or at a place other than where the records are maintained if that time or place would be more convenient for the employee. Nothing in this Act shall be construed as a requirement that an employee be permitted to remove any part of such personnel records or any part of such records from the place on the employer's premises where it is made available for inspection. Each employer shall retain the right to protect his records from loss, damage, or alteration to insure the integrity of the records. If an employee demonstrates that he or she is unable to review his or her personnel record at the employing unit, the employer shall, upon the employee's written request, mail a copy of the requested record to the employee.

§ 3. Copies. After the review time provided in Section 2, an employee may obtain a copy of the information or part of the information contained in the employee's personnel record. An employer may charge a fee for providing a copy of such information. The fee shall be limited to the actual cost of duplicating the information.

§ 4. Personnel record information which was not included in the personnel record but should have been as required by this Act shall not be used by an employer in a judicial or quasi-judicial proceeding. However, personnel record information which, in the opinion of the judge in a judicial proceeding or the hearing officer in a quasi-judicial proceeding, was not intentionally excluded from the personnel record may be used by the employer in the proceeding if the employee agrees or has been given a reasonable time to review the information. Material which should have been included in the personnel record shall be used at the request of the employee.

§ 5. Personnel Record Inspection by Representative. An employee who is involved in a current grievance against the employer may designate in writing a representative of the employee's union or collective bargaining unit or other representative to inspect the employee's personnel record which may have a bearing on the resolution of the grievance, except as provided in Section 10. The employer shall allow such a designated representative to inspect that employee's personnel record in the same manner as provided under Section 2.

§ 6. Personnel Record Correction. If the employee disagrees with any information contained in the personnel record, a removal or correction of that information may be mutually agreed upon by the employer and the employee. If an agreement cannot be reached, the employee may submit a written statement explaining the employee's position. The employer shall attach the employee's statement to the disputed portion of the personnel record. The employee's statement shall be included whenever that disputed portion of the personnel record is released to a third party as long as the disputed record is a part of the file. The inclusion of any written statement attached in the record without further comment or action by the employer, shall not imply or create any presumption of employer agreement with its contents. If either the employer or the employee knowingly places in the personnel record information which is false, the employer or employee, whichever is appropriate, shall have remedy through legal action to have that information expunged.

§7. (1) An employer or former employer shall not divulge a disciplinary report, letter of reprimand, or other disciplinary action to a third party, to a party who is not a part of the employer's organization, or to a party who is not a part of a labor organization representing the employee, without written notice as provided in this Section.

(2) The written notice to the employee shall be by first-class mail to the employee's last known address and shall be mailed on or before the day the information is divulged.

(3) This Section shall not apply if:
   (a) the employee has specifically waived written notice as part of a written, signed employment application with another employer;
   (b) the disclosure is ordered to a party in a legal action or arbitration; or
   (c) information is requested by a government agency as a result of a claim or complaint by an employee, or as a result of a criminal investigation by such agency.

(4) An employer who receives a request for records of a disciplinary report, letter of reprimand, or other disciplinary action in relation to an employee under the

Freedom of Information Act may provide notification to the employee in written form as described in subsection (2) or through electronic mail, if available.

§ 8. An employer shall review a personnel record before releasing information to a third party and, except when the release is ordered to a party in a legal action or arbitration, delete disciplinary reports, letters of reprimand, or other records of disciplinary action which are more than 4 years old.

§ 9. An employer shall not gather or keep a record of an employee's associations, political activities, publications, communications or nonemployment activities, unless the employee submits the information in writing or authorizes the employer in writing to keep or gather the information. This prohibition shall not apply to the activities that occur on the employer's premises or during the employee's working hours with that employer which interfere with the performance of the employee's duties or the duties of other employees or activities, regardless of when and where occurring, which constitute criminal conduct or may reasonably be expected to harm the employer's property, operations or business, or could by the employee's action cause the employer financial liability. A record which is kept by the employer as permitted under this Section shall be part of the personnel record.

§ 10. Exceptions. The right of the employee or the employee's designated representative to inspect his or her personnel records does not apply to:

(a) Letters of reference for that employee or external peer review documents for academic employees of institutions of higher education.

(b) Any portion of a test document, except that the employee may see a cumulative total test score for either a section of or the entire test document.

(c) Materials relating to the employer's staff planning, such as matters relating to the business' development, expansion, closing or operational goals, where the materials relate to or affect more than one employee, provided, however, that this exception does not apply if such materials are, have been or are intended to be used by the employer in determining an individual employee's qualifications for employment, promotion, transfer, or additional compensation, or in determining an individual employee's discharge or discipline.

(d) Information of a personal nature about a person other than the employee if disclosure of the information would constitute a clearly unwarranted invasion of the other person's privacy.

(e) An employer who does not maintain any personnel records.(f) Records relevant to any other pending claim between the employer and employee which may be discovered in a judicial proceeding.

(g) Investigatory or security records maintained by an employer to investigate criminal conduct by an employee or other activity by the employee which could reasonably be expected to harm the employer's property, operations, or business or could by the employee's activity cause the employer financial liability, unless and until the employer takes adverse personnel action based on information in such records.

§ 11. This Act shall not be construed to diminish a right of access to records already otherwise provided by law, provided that disclosure of performance evaluations under the Freedom of Information Act shall be prohibited.

§ 12. (a) The Director of Labor or his authorized representative shall administer and enforce the provisions of this Act. The Director of Labor may issue rules and regulations necessary to administer and enforce the provisions of this Act.

(b) If an employee alleges that he or she has been denied his or her rights under this Act, he or she may file a complaint with the Department of Labor. The Department shall investigate the complaint and shall have authority to request the issuance of a search warrant or subpoena to inspect the files of the employer, if necessary. The Department shall attempt to resolve the complaint by conference, conciliation, or persuasion. If the complaint is not so resolved and the Department finds the employer has violated the Act, the Department may commence an action in the circuit court to enforce the provisions of this Act including an action to compel compliance. The circuit court for the county in which the complainant resides, in which the complainant is employed, or in which the personnel record is maintained shall have jurisdiction in such actions.

(c) If an employer violates this Act, an employee may commence an action in the circuit court to enforce the provisions of this Act, including actions to compel compliance, where efforts to resolve the employee's complaint concerning such violation by conference, conciliation or persuasion pursuant to subsection (b) have failed and the Department has not commenced an action in circuit court to redress such violation. The circuit court for the county in which the complainant resides, in which the complainant is employed, or in which the personnel record is maintained shall have jurisdiction in such actions.

(d) Failure to comply with an order of the court may be punished as contempt. In addition, the court shall award an employee prevailing in an action pursuant to this Act the following damages:

(1) Actual damages plus costs.

(2) For a willful and knowing violation of this Act, $200 plus costs, reasonable attorney's fees, and actual damages.

(e) Any employer or his agent who violates the provisions of this Act is guilty of a petty offense.

(f) Any employer or his agent, or the officer or agent of any private employer, who discharges or in any other manner discriminates against any employee because that employee has made a complaint to his employer, or to the Director or his authorized representative, or because that employee has caused to be instituted or is about to cause to be instituted any proceeding under or related to this Act, or because that employee has testified or is about to testify in an investigation or proceeding under this Act, is guilty of a petty offense.

§ 13. An employer shall not gather or keep a record identifying an employee as the subject of an investigation by the Department of Children and Family Services if the investigation by the Department of Children and Family Services resulted in an unfounded report as specified in the Abused and Neglected Child Reporting Act.

An employee upon receiving written notification from the Department of Children and Family Services that an investigation has resulted in an unfounded report shall take the written notification to his or her employer and have any record of the investigation expunged from his or her employee record.

Additional Reference Materials

(All referenced Illinois materials can be found on the Illinois General Assembly website at www.ilga.gov. Links to the federal materials are provided below.)

Illinois Laws:

1) Employee Credit Privacy Act [820 ILCS 70/1, *et seq.*]
2) Whistleblower Act [740 ILCS 174/1, *et seq.*]
3) Equal Pay Act of 2003 [820 ILCS 112/1, *et seq.*]
4) Human Rights Act [775 ILCS 5/1, *et seq.*]
5) State Officials and Employees Ethics Act [5 ILCS 430/1-1, *et seq.*]
6) Right to Breastfeed Act [740 ILCS 137/1, *et seq.*]
7) School Visitation Rights Act [820 ILCS 141/1, *et seq.*]

Federal Laws:

1) Americans with Disabilities Act [42 USC 12101, *et seq.*] www.ada.gov
2) Family and Medical Leave Act [29 USC 2601, *et seq.*] www.dol.gov/whd/flma

INDEX

A
Americans with Disabilities Act... 157
Animals on school property.. 15

B
Biometric information (student).. 52
Birth certificate... 26
Bus – see school bus

C
Certified staff (working with)... 11
Communication (establishing)... 12
Copyright laws.. 12
Course and scope of duties.. 3
Credit cards... 130

D
Dental examinations (student).. 92, 96
Diabetic students... 73
Discipline (employee)... 157
Divorced parents.. 51

E
Electronic grade books... 52
Emergency medical aid to students....................................... 73
Employee Credit Privacy Act... 158
Employment (issues related to)
    conflicts of interest.. 160
    email (use of school district)....................................... 160
    evaluation... 156
    discipline.. 157
    nursing mothers.. 157
    outside employment... 160
    overtime compensation... 157
    personnel records.. 156
    prohibited political activities...................................... 159
    religious holidays.. 157
    whistleblower protection... 158
    workplace harassment.. 157
Etiquette... 9
Equal Pay Act.. 159
Evaluation (employee)... 156
Eye examinations (student).. 92, 96

F

Family and Medical Leave Act	158
Fee waivers	114
Fire and safety drills (required)	13
Foster children	28, 115, 122
Free and reduced-price meals	114
Freedom of Information Act	12
Freedom of religion	117

G

Gift Ban Act	159

H

Harassment (workplace)	157
Health examination (student)	91, 96
Homeless students	
definition of	27, 115
generally	27, 115
homeless liaison	115
immunization and health exam	93
school attendance	27
transportation	115, 138
Homeschooling	
athletic participation	116
driver's education	116
generally	116
returning to school	116
special education students	116
textbooks and academic materials	116

I

Illegal aliens (right to education)	28, 115
Immunity from liability	4
Immunizations (student)	92, 96

J, K, L

Lawsuit (basics of a)	1
Low income students	114
free and reduced-price meals	114
textbook and fee waivers	114

M

Mandated reporter status	4
Medication	
administration at school	72

    generally 71
    prescription v. non-prescription. 72
    self-administration by students 73, 77
    storage 73
Military families. 28
Money management (basic) 127

N
Nursing mothers (in the workplace). 157

O
Overtime compensation 157

P
Personnel records 156
Petty cash 129
Phone calls 9
Prohibited political activities 159
Procurement cards 130
Public (dealing with) 11

Q, R
Reasonable employee 2
Religious holidays (employee) 157
Religious needs (student) 117
Residency (proof of). 26
Response to Intervention 113
Revolving fund accounts 129

S
Safety 10
School bus
    accident report. 140
    communication devices 139
    eating and drinking on a 142
    inspections. 139
    seat belts (use of). 142
School Visitation Act 159
Section 504 Plans
    differences from special education 113
    generally 112
    rights of parents. 113
Sex offenders at school. 14
Sexual harassment (workplace) 157

Special education
    differences from Section 504 113
    generally 111
    graduation 112
    graduation and transitional services 112
    homeschool students 115
    IEP 112
    IEP team 112
    residency 28
Student activity accounts 128
Student in good standing form 26
Student records
    categories of 52
    copies 50
    destruction 53
    former students (records of) 52
    military access 52
    parent's right to access 48
    record release 50, 60
    records custodian 50
    safeguarding 49
    student record access log 50, 60
    students who are 18 51
    transfer of records 50

T
Textbook waivers 114
Transportation
    allowable forms of 137
    bus inspections 139
    homeless students 138
    reimbursement 138
    students with disabilities 139
Truancy 30
Tuition (for not resident students) 29

U, V
Undocumented students 28, 115
Visitors 10

W, X, Y, Z
Whistleblower protection 158
Withdrawal from school 30
Workplace harassment 157